BEAUTIFUL PLATTERS

&

DELICIOUS BOARDS

BEAUTIFUL PLATTERS & DELICIOUS BOARDS

13-Digit ISBN: 978-1-64643-083-3
10-Digit ISBN: 1-64643-083-2

This book may be ordered by mail from the publisher. Please include $5.99 for postage and handling.
Please support your local bookseller first!

Books published by Cider Mill Press Book Publishers are available at special discounts for bulk purchases in the United States by corporations, institutions, and other organizations. For more information, please contact the publisher.

Cider Mill Press Book Publishers
"Where good books are ready for press"
PO Box 454
12 Spring Street
Kennebunkport, Maine 04046

Visit us online!
cidermillpress.com

Typography: Archer, Brandon Grotesque, Gotham

Image Credits: Photos on pages 18, 21, 30, 35, 53, 78, 80-81, 85, 93, 105, 118, 121, 123, 139, 161, 170, 194-195, 199, 200, 203, 211, 215, 220, 227, 235, and 247 courtesy of Cider Mill Press Book Publishers.
Photo on page 37 © StockFood / Katarzyna, Kachel. Photo on page 150 © StockFood / The Stepford Husband.
All other images used under official license from Shutterstock.com.

Back cover images:
Herb-Encrusted Goat Cheese, see page 43, Roasted Beet Spread, see page 51, Apricot & Chili Jam, see page 96, Bacon & Zucchini Quiche, see page 222, Whoopie Pies, see page 184, Stuffed Peppers, see page 76, Rosemary & Thyme Focaccia, see page 20, Guacamole, see page 107.

Printed in China
4 5 6 7 8 9 0

BEAUTIFUL PLATTERS
&
DELICIOUS BOARDS

Over 150 Recipes and Tips for Crafting
Memorable Serving Boards

CIDER MILL PRESS

BOOK
PUBLISHERS
KENNEBUNKPORT, MAINE

CONTENTS

INTRODUCTION 7

SPRING 10

SUMMER 70

FALL 132

WINTER 194

INDEX 251

A MOVEABLE FEAST

WHEN THE SERVING BOARD COMES OUT, it means something special is about to happen. It may seem impossible looking at it, but that humble wooden board can quickly become the most extravagant element on a table, or in a room. A cleverly composed serving board can turn a boring spread into a "wow" moment for friends and family.

Whether it is a gorgeous assortment of cheeses preceding a formal dinner party, or a simple afternoon nibble of nuts and sliced fruit to go with a glass of chilled Rosé, serving anything on a board instantly elevates the moment. Large or small, round or rectangular, unfinished or varnished, a board can take many forms. But no matter what, it is always a welcome sight.

Traditionally, it is used to showcase something beautiful: a few perfect tomatoes from the garden, a wedge of cheese recommended by a local cheese monger, or a luxurious pile of cured meat. Whether it is presenting these, a loaf of bread fresh from the oven, olives a friend brought back from their travels, or a beautiful handmade preserve and a handful of crackers you baked yourself, the serving board is a blank canvas, made to let you craft, slice, and display limitless combinations of foodstuffs that suit your tastes and moods.

That freewheeling nature, which is at the center of so much of the excitement that builds around the serving board, can also make it difficult to know what exactly should go on a board. To make it easier, we've picked out some of our favorite boards to serve as sources of inspiration, and a number of excellent recipes that will help you curate the perfect collection of bites.

So break out those boards, and proceed boldly. And if you do get stuck, just flip through these pages until you find a solution.

SPRING

Making it through another winter in one piece is enough cause for celebration. But too often, our relief at what has passed eclipses the brilliance that is unfurling right under our noses. As the world moves into the season of regeneration, we recommend taking some time to sit back and appreciate the miracle that arrives at the end of each and every winter: spring.

What better way to ensure that you take this time than a series of beautiful boards marking the occasion? Sitting around with your loved ones and enjoying delicious food as you gaze out at the world coming back to life, you can't help but become a little more optimistic about what the future holds.

YIELD: 6 CRACKERS
ACTIVE TIME: 15 MINUTES
TOTAL TIME: 1 HOUR AND 10 MINUTES

ROSEMARY CRACKERS

⅛ TEASPOON ACTIVE
DRY YEAST

1 TABLESPOON LUKEWARM
WATER (90°F)

¾ CUP ALL-PURPOSE FLOUR,
PLUS MORE AS NEEDED

½ TEASPOON KOSHER SALT

PINCH OF SUGAR

1 TABLESPOON FINELY
CHOPPED FRESH ROSEMARY

OLIVE OIL, AS NEEDED

1 Preheat the oven to 350°F.

2 Place the yeast and the warm water in a mixing bowl, stir gently, and let stand for 10 minutes.

3 Add the remaining ingredients, except for the olive oil, to the bowl and knead the mixture until it is a smooth dough.

4 Cover the bowl with a kitchen towel and let it stand in a naturally warm spot for 15 to 20 minutes, until the dough doubles in size.

5 Place the dough on a lightly flour-dusted work surface and roll it out as thin as you can without it tearing.

6 Cut the dough into the desired shapes and place them on a parchment-lined baking sheet. Brush the top of each cracker with a small amount of olive oil.

7 Place the crackers in the oven and bake for 20 minutes, or until golden brown. Remove and let the crackers cool on a wire rack before serving.

YIELD: 8 CRISPS

ACTIVE TIME: 10 MINUTES

TOTAL TIME: 10 MINUTES

PARMESAN CRISPS

½ CUP GRATED
PARMESAN CHEESE

1 Preheat the oven to 400°F.

2 Place a tablespoon of Parmesan on a parchment-lined baking sheet and gently pat it down to flatten. Repeat with the remaining cheese, spacing the tablespoons about ½ inch apart.

3 Place in the oven and bake for 3 to 5 minutes, or until golden brown and crisp. Remove from the oven and let the crisps cool on a wire rack before serving.

YIELD: 4 TO 6 SERVINGS
ACTIVE TIME: 15 MINUTES
TOTAL TIME: 35 MINUTES

CROSTINI WITH RICOTTA & PEA SHOOTS

1 BAGUETTE, SLICED

7 TABLESPOONS OLIVE OIL, PLUS MORE TO TASTE

3 CUPS WHOLE MILK RICOTTA CHEESE

½ TEASPOON SEA SALT, PLUS MORE TO TASTE

½ TEASPOON BLACK PEPPER, PLUS MORE TO TASTE

3 GARLIC CLOVES, MINCED

3 TABLESPOONS FINELY CHOPPED FRESH MINT

1 TABLESPOON LEMON ZEST

PEA SHOOTS, FOR GARNISH

1   Preheat the oven to 400°F. Brush the slices of baguette with 1 tablespoon of the olive oil and place them on a baking sheet. Place in the oven and bake for 12 to 15 minutes, turning the slices over halfway through. When the slices are golden brown on both sides, remove from the oven.

2   Place the ricotta, the remaining olive oil, salt, and pepper in a bowl and stir until the mixture is light and fluffy. Stir in the garlic, mint, and lemon zest. Spread the ricotta mixture on the baguette slices.

3   Drizzle olive oil over the crostini and sprinkle sea salt and black pepper on top. Top with the pea shoots and serve.

YIELD: 4 SERVINGS

ACTIVE TIME: 30 MINUTES

TOTAL TIME: 1 HOUR AND 15 MINUTES

DEEP-FRIED OYSTERS

1 CUP CANOLA OIL

1 CUP CORNMEAL

SALT, TO TASTE

½ LB. OYSTER MEAT

2 EGGS, BEATEN

1 TABLESPOON UNSALTED BUTTER

4 KING'S HAWAIIAN ROLLS, HALVED

1 Place the oil in a Dutch oven and bring it to 350°F over medium-high heat. Place the cornmeal and salt in a bowl and stir to combine.

2 When the oil is ready, dip an oyster into the beaten eggs and then into the cornmeal-and-salt mixture. Repeat until all of the oysters are evenly coated.

3 Place the oysters in the oil and fry until golden brown, about 3 to 5 minutes. Remove from the oil and set on a paper towel–lined plate to drain.

4 Place the butter in a skillet and melt over medium heat. Place the buns in the skillet and toast until lightly browned. Remove, top with the fried oysters, and serve.

YIELD: 12 SERVINGS

ACTIVE TIME: 30 MINUTES

TOTAL TIME: 26 HOURS

ROSEMARY & THYME FOCACCIA

3¼ CUPS ALL-PURPOSE FLOUR

1½ CUPS WATER (78°F)

½ TEASPOON ACTIVE DRY YEAST

1 TABLESPOON KOSHER SALT

¼ CUP OLIVE OIL, PLUS MORE AS NEEDED

3 GARLIC CLOVES, SLICED THIN

LEAVES FROM 2 SPRIGS OF FRESH ROSEMARY

LEAVES FROM 2 SPRIGS OF FRESH THYME

1   Place the flour, water, and yeast in a large bowl and stir to combine. Mix well with your hands to ensure that all of the flour, salt, and yeast is incorporated.

2   Cover the bowl and let it sit in a naturally warm place overnight, giving the dough time to come together and develop flavor. The dough should double in size.

3   After the dough has rested, preheat the oven to 450°F and grease a baking sheet with olive oil.

4   Place the dough on the baking sheet and pat it into a ½-inch-thick rectangle. Brush the focaccia with the olive oil and sprinkle the garlic, rosemary, and thyme on top.

5   Place in the oven and bake until golden brown, about 20 to 30 minutes. Remove and let cool slightly before serving.

PITA BREAD

2¼ TEASPOONS ACTIVE
DRY YEAST

2½ CUPS LUKEWARM
WATER (90°F)

3 CUPS ALL-PURPOSE FLOUR,
PLUS MORE AS NEEDED

2 TABLESPOONS OLIVE OIL

1 TABLESPOON KOSHER SALT

3 CUPS WHOLE WHEAT FLOUR

BUTTER, AS NEEDED

1   Place the yeast and the water in a bowl and gently stir. Let the mixture sit until it starts to foam, about 10 minutes.

2   Place the yeast mixture in a large mixing bowl. Add the all-purpose flour and stir until a stiff dough forms. Cover the bowl with plastic wrap and let the dough rise for about 1 hour.

3   Add 1 tablespoon of the oil and the salt to the dough and knead to incorporate. Incorporate the whole wheat flour in ½-cup increments and then stir until the dough is soft. Place the dough on a flour-dusted work surface and knead until it is smooth and elastic, about 10 minutes.

4   Grease a large mixing bowl with butter. Place the ball of dough in the bowl, cover loosely with plastic wrap, place in a naturally warm spot, and let it rise until doubled in size, about 45 minutes to 1 hour.

5   Place the dough on a flour-dusted work surface, punch it down, and cut it into 16 pieces. Place the pieces on a baking sheet and cover with a damp kitchen towel while working with individual pieces. Roll out the pieces with a rolling pin until they are approximately 7 inches in diameter. Stack the pitas, placing sheets of plastic wrap between them.

6   Warm a cast-iron skillet over high heat and add the remaining olive oil. Working with one pita at a time, cook for about 20 seconds on one side, then flip and cook for a minute on the other side, until bubbles form. Turn over again and cook until the pita puffs up, another minute or so. Store the cooked pitas under a kitchen towel until ready to serve.

YIELD: 2 CUPS

ACTIVE TIME: 10 MINUTES

TOTAL TIME: 45 MINUTES

SPICED ALMONDS

4 TABLESPOONS UNSALTED
BUTTER, MELTED

4 TEASPOONS
WORCESTERSHIRE SAUCE

1 TEASPOON CUMIN

2 TEASPOONS CHILI POWDER

1 TEASPOON GARLIC POWDER

½ TEASPOON ONION POWDER

1 TEASPOON CAYENNE PEPPER

1 TEASPOON KOSHER SALT

2 CUPS WHOLE ALMONDS

1 Preheat the oven to 350°F and line a baking sheet with parchment paper.

2 Place all of the ingredients, except for the almonds, in a mixing bowl and stir until combined. Add the almonds and toss to coat.

3 Transfer the almonds to the baking sheet, place it in the oven, and roast for about 15 minutes, until the almonds are a darker brown and fragrant. Turn the almonds over occasionally as they roast. Remove and let cool before serving.

YIELD: 6 SERVINGS
ACTIVE TIME: 5 MINUTES
TOTAL TIME: 5 MINUTES

OYSTERS WITH MIGNONETTE SAUCE

12 TO 24 OYSTERS, SHUCKED

1½ TABLESPOONS MINCED SHALLOT

⅓ CUP RED WINE VINEGAR

1½ TABLESPOONS CRUSHED BLACK PEPPER

SALT, TO TASTE

1 Arrange the oysters on a platter filled with ice. Place the remaining ingredients in a small bowl and stir to combine.

YIELD: 6 SERVINGS

ACTIVE TIME: 30 MINUTES

TOTAL TIME: 2 HOURS

SPANISH POTATO TORTILLA

5 LARGE RUSSET POTATOES, PEELED AND SLICED THIN

1 SPANISH ONION, SLICED

½ CUP VEGETABLE OIL, PLUS MORE AS NEEDED

½ CUP OLIVE OIL

10 EGGS, AT ROOM TEMPERATURE

GENEROUS PINCH OF KOSHER SALT

1 Place the potatoes, onion, vegetable oil, and olive oil in a 12-inch cast-iron skillet. The potatoes should be submerged. If not, add more vegetable oil as needed. Bring to a gentle simmer over low heat and cook until the potatoes are tender, about 30 minutes. Remove from heat and let cool slightly.

2 Use a slotted spoon to remove the potatoes and onion from the oil. Reserve the oil. Place the eggs and salt in a large bowl and whisk to combine. Add the potatoes and onion to the eggs.

3 Warm the skillet over high heat. Add ¼ cup of the reserved oil and swirl to coat the bottom and sides of the pan. Pour the egg-and-potato mixture into the pan and stir vigorously to ensure that the mixture does not stick to the sides. Cook for 1 minute and remove from heat. Place the pan over low heat, cover, and cook for 3 minutes.

4 Carefully invert the tortilla onto a large plate. Return it to the skillet, cook for 3 minutes, and then invert it onto the plate. Return it to the skillet and cook for another 3 minutes. Remove the tortilla from the pan and let it rest at room temperature for 1 hour before serving.

YIELD: 6 SERVINGS

ACTIVE TIME: 30 MINUTES

TOTAL TIME: 1 HOUR AND 30 MINUTES

DUDHI KOFTA

2 LBS. ZUCCHINI, TRIMMED AND GRATED

2 TEASPOONS KOSHER SALT

1 SMALL RED ONION, CHOPPED

¼ CUP RAW CASHEWS

2 GARLIC CLOVES, MINCED

1-INCH PIECE OF FRESH GINGER, PEELED AND MINCED

4 BIRD'S EYE CHILI PEPPERS, STEMMED, SEEDED, AND MINCED

½ CUP CHICKPEA FLOUR

2 TABLESPOONS FINELY CHOPPED FRESH CILANTRO

4 CUPS VEGETABLE OIL

1   Place the grated zucchini in a bowl, add the salt, and stir to combine. Let stand for 20 minutes.

2   Place the onion, cashews, garlic, ginger, and chilies in a food processor and blitz until the mixture becomes a chunky paste.

3   Place the zucchini in a kitchen towel and wring it to remove as much liquid as possible. Place the zucchini in a mixing bowl and add the onion-and-cashew paste. Stir to combine, add the chickpea flour and cilantro, and fold to incorporate. The dough should be slightly wet.

4   Place the vegetable oil in a Dutch oven and heat it to 300°F. As the oil warms, form tablespoons of the dough into balls and place them on a parchment-lined baking sheet. When the oil is ready, place the dumplings in the oil and fry until golden brown, about 5 minutes. Work in batches if necessary. Transfer the cooked dumplings to a paper towel–lined plate to drain before serving.

YIELD: 4 SERVINGS

ACTIVE TIME: 30 MINUTES

TOTAL TIME: 2 HOURS AND 30 MINUTES

POLENTA FRIES

2½ CUPS MILK

2½ CUPS VEGETABLE STOCK

2 CUPS MEDIUM-GRAIN CORNMEAL

2 TABLESPOONS UNSALTED BUTTER

1 TEASPOON KOSHER SALT, PLUS MORE TO TASTE

½ TEASPOON BLACK PEPPER

½ TEASPOON DRIED OREGANO

½ TEASPOON DRIED THYME

½ TEASPOON DRIED ROSEMARY

4 CUPS VEGETABLE OIL

¼ CUP GRATED PARMESAN CHEESE, FOR GARNISH

2 TABLESPOONS FINELY CHOPPED FRESH ROSEMARY, FOR GARNISH

1   Grease a large, rimmed baking sheet with nonstick cooking spray. Place the milk and stock in a saucepan and bring to a boil. Whisk in the cornmeal, reduce heat to low and cook, while stirring constantly, until all of the liquid has been absorbed and the polenta is creamy, about 5 minutes.

2   Stir in the butter, salt, pepper, oregano, thyme, and rosemary. When they have been incorporated, transfer the polenta to the greased baking sheet and even out the surface with a rubber spatula. Refrigerate for 2 hours.

3   Carefully invert the baking sheet over a cutting board so that the polenta falls onto it. Slice in half lengthwise and cut each piece into 4-inch-long and 1-inch-wide strips.

4   Place the oil in a Dutch oven and bring it to 375°F. Working in batches of two, place the strips in the oil and fry, turning as they cook, until golden brown, 2 to 4 minutes. Transfer the cooked fries to a paper towel–lined plate to drain. When all of the fries have been cooked, sprinkle the Parmesan and rosemary over them and serve.

CORNISH PASTIES

FOR THE DOUGH

3 CUPS ALL-PURPOSE FLOUR, PLUS MORE AS NEEDED

¾ TEASPOON KOSHER SALT

½ CUP LARD OR UNSALTED BUTTER, CUT INTO SMALL PIECES

1 LARGE EGG, BEATEN

¼ CUP COLD WATER, PLUS MORE AS NEEDED

2 TEASPOONS DISTILLED WHITE VINEGAR

Continued...

1   To prepare the dough, place the flour and salt in a bowl, add the lard or butter, and use a pastry blender to work the mixture until it is coarse crumbs. Beat the egg, water, and vinegar together in a separate bowl and then drizzle this mixture over the flour mixture. Use the pastry blender to work the mixture until it starts to hold together. Knead the dough with your hands, adding water in 1-teaspoon increments if it is too dry. Cut the dough into 6 pieces, cover with plastic wrap, and chill in the refrigerator.

2   Preheat the oven to 400°F and prepare the filling. Place all of the ingredients, except for the egg and water, in a bowl and stir to combine. Place the egg and water in a separate bowl and beat to combine.

3   Place the pieces of dough on a flour-dusted work surface, roll each one into an 8-inch circle, and place ½ cup of the filling in the center of each circle. Brush the edge of each circle with water, fold into a half-moon, and crimp the edge to seal. Place the sealed handpies on a parchment-lined baking sheet.

4   Brush the pastries with the egg wash and use a paring knife to make a small incision in the side of each one. Bake in the oven for 15 minutes, reduce the temperature to 350°F, and bake for another 25 minutes. Remove from the oven and let cool on a wire rack before serving.

FOR THE FILLING

¾ LB. SKIRT STEAK,
CUT INTO ½-INCH CUBES

¼ CUP PEELED AND
CHOPPED PARSNIPS

¼ CUP PEELED AND
CHOPPED TURNIPS

1 SMALL ONION, CHOPPED

1 CUP PEELED AND
CHOPPED POTATO

1 TABLESPOON FINELY
CHOPPED FRESH THYME

2 TABLESPOONS
TOMATO PASTE

SALT AND PEPPER, TO TASTE

1 LARGE EGG, BEATEN

1 TABLESPOON WATER

YIELD: 8 SERVINGS

ACTIVE TIME: 20 MINUTES

TOTAL TIME: 2 HOURS

ASPARAGUS QUICHE

2 CUPS CHOPPED ASPARAGUS

1 PIECRUST, BLIND BAKED (SEE BELOW)

6 LARGE EGGS

2 LARGE EGG YOLKS

1 CUP CRÈME FRAÎCHE

½ CUP MILK

½ CUP HEAVY CREAM

1 CUP GRATED CHEDDAR CHEESE

½ TEASPOON KOSHER SALT

¼ TEASPOON BLACK PEPPER

½ CUP FROZEN PEAS

2 TABLESPOONS FRESH MINT LEAVES, FOR GARNISH

1 Preheat the oven to 350°F. Bring water to a boil in a large saucepan and prepare an ice water bath. Place the asparagus in the boiling water for 15 seconds, transfer to the ice water bath, and let it sit for 2 minutes. Drain, pat the asparagus dry, and distribute the pieces in the piecrust.

2 Place the eggs, egg yolks, crème fraîche, milk, cream, cheese, salt, and pepper in a mixing bowl, stir to combine, and then stir in the peas. Pour the mixture into the crust and gently shake the pie plate to distribute evenly.

3 Place the quiche in the oven and bake until it is puffy and golden brown, about 35 minutes. Remove, let cool for 10 minutes, and garnish with the mint leaves before serving.

BLIND BAKING

The technique of baking a piecrust before filling it is also known as "blind baking." When working with a custard filling, as in a lemon meringue or pumpkin pie, baking the crust prevents pockets of steam from forming in the crust once it is filled, which can cause the crust to become puffy and uneven. Blind baking also keeps the bottom of the crust from becoming soggy.

Uncooked rice is the most typical weight when blind baking a pie, though dried beans and weights designed specifically for the task can also be utilized. To blind bake a crust, place it in a pie plate, fill it with your chosen weight, place in a 350°F oven, and bake for 15 to 20 minutes, until it is golden brown and firm. Remove and let cool completely before filling.

CANNING 101

1   Bring a pot of water to a boil. Place your mason jars in the water for 15 to 20 minutes to sterilize them. Do not boil the mason jar lids, as this can prevent them from creating a proper seal when the time comes.

2   Bring water to a boil in the large canning pot. Fill the sterilized mason jars with whatever you are canning. Place the lids on the jars and secure the bands tightly. Place the jars in the boiling water for 40 minutes. Use a pair of canning tongs to remove the jars from the boiling water and let them cool. As they are cooling, you should hear the classic "ping and pop" sound of the lids creating a seal.

3   After 6 hours, check the lids. There should be no give in them and they should be suctioned onto the jars. Discard any lids and food that did not seal properly.

BREAD & BUTTER PICKLES

2 PERSIAN CUCUMBERS,
SLICED THIN

1 SMALL ONION, SLICED THIN

2 JALAPEÑO PEPPERS,
SLICED THIN

4 SPRIGS OF FRESH DILL

2 TABLESPOONS
CORIANDER SEEDS

2 TABLESPOONS
MUSTARD SEEDS

2 TEASPOONS CELERY SALT

2 CUPS DISTILLED
WHITE VINEGAR

1 CUP SUGAR

2 TABLESPOONS KOSHER SALT

1 Place the cucumbers, onion, jalapeños, dill, coriander seeds, mustard seeds, and celery salt in a sterilized 1-quart mason jar.

2 Place the vinegar, sugar, and salt in a medium saucepan and bring it to a boil, while stirring to dissolve the sugar and salt. Carefully pour the brine into the jar, filling all the way to the top. If you want to can these pickles, see the sidebar on the opposite page. If you do not want to can the pickles, let the mixture cool completely before sealing and storing in the refrigerator, where they will keep for up to 1 week.

YIELD: 8 SERVINGS

ACTIVE TIME: 15 MINUTES

TOTAL TIME: 20 MINUTES

EGGPLANT SPREAD

1 LB. EGGPLANT

2 GARLIC CLOVES, DICED

¼ CUP TAHINI

½ TEASPOON FRESH
LEMON JUICE

1 TEASPOON KOSHER SALT

½ TEASPOON CUMIN

½ TEASPOON PAPRIKA

¼ TEASPOON
CAYENNE PEPPER

2 TABLESPOONS OLIVE OIL

1 TABLESPOON FINELY
CHOPPED FRESH PARSLEY,
FOR GARNISH

1 Preheat the oven to 400°F. Pierce the skin of the eggplant with a knife or fork and place it on a baking sheet. Place it in the oven and roast for about 25 minutes, until the skin is blistered and the flesh is tender. Remove from the oven and let cool.

2 Peel the eggplant and chop the flesh. Place it in a bowl with the remaining ingredients, except for the parsley, and stir to combine. Garnish with the parsley and serve.

TIP: For a creamier texture, use a food processor or blender to puree the eggplant before adding the rest of the ingredients.

YIELD: 4 SERVINGS

ACTIVE TIME: 10 MINUTES

TOTAL TIME: 1 HOUR AND 10 MINUTES

HERB-ENCRUSTED GOAT CHEESE

½ LB. LOG OF GOAT CHEESE

2 TABLESPOONS FINELY CHOPPED FRESH TARRAGON

2 TABLESPOONS FINELY CHOPPED FRESH CHIVES

2 TABLESPOONS FINELY CHOPPED FRESH THYME

1 CUP OLIVE OIL

CRUSTY BREAD, FOR SERVING

CRACKERS, FOR SERVING

1 Slice the goat cheese into thick rounds. Gently roll the rounds in the herbs and gently press down so that the herbs adhere to the surface of the cheese.

2 Layer the rounds in mason jars. Pour the olive oil over them until they are covered. Let the mixture sit for an hour before serving with crusty bread or crackers.

STRAWBERRY & RHUBARB CHUTNEY

2 TABLESPOONS OLIVE OIL

¼ CUP DICED RED ONION

2 GARLIC CLOVES, GRATED

1-INCH PIECE OF FRESH
GINGER, PEELED AND MINCED

5 RHUBARB STALKS, TRIMMED
AND SLICED THIN

1 CUP WHITE WINE

SEEDS FROM 3 CARDAMOM
PODS, GROUND

5 WHOLE CLOVES, GROUND

1 TEASPOON BLACK PEPPER

¼ CUP SUGAR

2 TABLESPOONS FRESH
LIME JUICE

2 TABLESPOONS APPLE
CIDER VINEGAR

1 PINT OF STRAWBERRIES

1 Place olive oil in a saucepan and warm over medium heat. Add the red onion and cook for 1 minute, then stir in the garlic, ginger, and rhubarb. Cook, while stirring frequently, until the onion and rhubarb start to soften, about 5 minutes.

2 Deglaze the pan with the white wine and let the alcohol cook off for 1 minute. Add the spices, sugar, lime juice, and vinegar and cook until the mixture starts to thicken.

3 Add the strawberries and cook, while mashing the mixture with a wooden spoon, for about 2 minutes. Season to taste, remove from heat, and let cool completely before serving.

YIELD: 8 CHEESE BALLS

ACTIVE TIME: 15 MINUTES

TOTAL TIME: 1 HOUR AND 30 MINUTES

BACON CHEESE BALLS

6 OZ. FROMAGE BLANC CHEESE

3 OZ. AGED CHEDDAR CHEESE, GRATED

3 OZ. BLUE CHEESE, CRUMBLED

½ TABLESPOON SOUR CREAM

1 TO 2 DASHES WORCESTERSHIRE SAUCE

¼ TEASPOON GARLIC POWDER

¼ TEASPOON BLACK PEPPER

PINCH OF KOSHER SALT

2 SCALLIONS, TRIMMED AND SLICED THIN

1 CUP COOKED AND CHOPPED BACON

1 Place the cheeses, sour cream, Worcestershire sauce, garlic powder, pepper, and salt in a food processor or blender and puree until the mixture is smooth.

2 Place the mixture in a large bowl, fold in the scallions, and divide the mixture into eight evenly sized balls. Place them on a parchment-lined baking sheet and refrigerate for 1 hour.

3 Place the bacon in a skillet and cook over medium heat until it is crisp, about 8 minutes. Place on a paper towel–lined plate to drain and then place on a piece of waxed paper.

4 Roll the cheese balls in the bacon until evenly coated and then serve.

YIELD: 1 CUP

ACTIVE TIME: 5 MINUTES

TOTAL TIME: 5 MINUTES

CILANTRO & MINT CHUTNEY

1 CUP FIRMLY PACKED
FRESH CILANTRO

½ CUP FIRMLY PACKED
FRESH MINT LEAVES

¼ CUP CHOPPED
WHITE ONION

3 TABLESPOONS WATER

1½ TEASPOONS FRESH
LIME JUICE

½ TEASPOON MINCED
SERRANO PEPPER

½ TEASPOON SUGAR

SALT, TO TASTE

1 Place all ingredients in a blender and pulse until combined. Take care not to overwork the mixture, as you want the chutney to have some texture.

ROASTED BEET SPREAD

4 BEETS, PEELED AND CUBED

¼ CUP OLIVE OIL

½ TEASPOON SEA SALT, PLUS MORE TO TASTE

¾ TEASPOON CUMIN SEEDS

¾ TEASPOON CORIANDER SEEDS

2 GARLIC CLOVES, MINCED, PLUS MORE TO TASTE

2 TEASPOONS MINCED GREEN CHILI PEPPER

2 TEASPOONS FRESH LEMON JUICE, PLUS MORE TO TASTE

⅓ CUP FINELY CHOPPED FRESH CILANTRO LEAVES

1 Preheat the oven to 400°F and line a baking sheet with parchment paper. Place the beets in a bowl with 2 tablespoons of the olive oil and ¼ teaspoon of the salt. Toss to coat.

2 Arrange the beets on the baking sheet in a single layer and roast for about 1 hour, stirring occasionally, until the beets are tender.

3 Toast the cumin and coriander seeds in a dry skillet over medium-high heat for about 2 minutes, stirring constantly, until they become fragrant and change color slightly. Be careful not to burn them or they will become bitter. Grind the seeds in a spice grinder or with a mortar and pestle.

4 Place the beets in a food processor and add the remaining olive oil and salt, the ground seeds, garlic, chili pepper, and lemon juice. Puree until smooth.

5 Taste and adjust the seasoning as needed. Transfer the dip to a bowl, stir in the cilantro, and serve.

YIELD: 2 CUPS
ACTIVE TIME: 15 MINUTES
TOTAL TIME: 15 MINUTES

PEA SHOOT PESTO

2 CUPS PEA SHOOTS

1 CUP FRESH BASIL LEAVES

2 TABLESPOONS FRESH
LEMON JUICE

½ TEASPOON RED
PEPPER FLAKES

¼ CUP PINE NUTS

¼ CUP GRATED
PARMESAN CHEESE

¼ CUP OLIVE OIL

SALT AND PEPPER, TO TASTE

1　Place the pea shoots, basil, lemon juice, red pepper flakes, pine nuts, and Parmesan in a food processor and pulse until the mixture is a coarse paste. Gradually incorporate the olive oil as you continue to pulse the mixture.

2　Season with salt and pepper and serve. The pesto will keep in the refrigerator for 3 days.

YIELD: 4 CUPS
ACTIVE TIME: 15 MINUTES
TOTAL TIME: 35 MINUTES

TABBOULEH

½ CUP BULGUR WHEAT

1½ CUPS BOILING WATER

½ TEASPOON KOSHER SALT, PLUS MORE TO TASTE

½ CUP FRESH LEMON JUICE

2 CUPS FRESH PARSLEY, CHOPPED

1 CUP PEELED, SEEDED, AND DICED CUCUMBER

1 TOMATO, DICED

¼ CUP SLICED SCALLIONS

1 CUP FRESH MINT LEAVES, CHOPPED

2 TABLESPOONS OLIVE OIL

BLACK PEPPER, TO TASTE

½ CUP CRUMBLED FETA CHEESE

1   Place the bulgur in a heatproof bowl and add the boiling water, salt, and half of the lemon juice. Cover and let sit for about 20 minutes, until the bulgur has absorbed the water and is tender. Drain any excess water if necessary. Let the bulgur cool completely.

2   When the bulgur is completely cooled, add the parsley, cucumber, tomato, scallions, mint, olive oil, black pepper, and remaining lemon juice. Taste and add more salt if necessary.

3   When ready to serve, place on a plate and top with the feta.

YIELD: 4 SERVINGS

ACTIVE TIME: 20 MINUTES

TOTAL TIME: 30 MINUTES

SHIITAKE SPREAD

1 TABLESPOON OLIVE OIL

½ CUP MINCED SHALLOTS

1 GARLIC CLOVE, MINCED

¾ LB. SHIITAKE MUSHROOM CAPS, CHOPPED

SALT, TO TASTE

1 TABLESPOON SHERRY

¼ CUP HEAVY CREAM

LEAVES FROM 2 SPRIGS OF FRESH THYME

3 TABLESPOONS GRATED PARMESAN CHEESE

¼ CUP CREAM CHEESE, AT ROOM TEMPERATURE (OPTIONAL)

1 Place a large skillet over medium heat and add the oil. When it starts to shimmer, add the shallot and garlic and cook until the shallot starts to brown, about 5 to 7 minutes.

2 Add the mushrooms and a pinch of salt and cook until the mushrooms have started to brown, about 8 minutes. Stir in the sherry and scrape the browned bits off the bottom of the pan.

3 Add the cream and thyme and continue to cook until the mixture has thickened to where it is almost a paste. Remove the pan from heat.

4 Add the Parmesan cheese, taste, and adjust the seasoning as needed. If adding cream cheese, let the mixture cool a little and then fold in the cream cheese until thoroughly combined.

YIELD: 1 CUP

ACTIVE TIME: 10 MINUTES

TOTAL TIME: 2 HOURS

CHILI HONEY

4 SPICY CHILI PEPPERS

1 CUP HONEY

1　Place the chili peppers and honey in a saucepan and bring to a very gentle simmer over medium-low heat. Reduce the heat to its lowest possible setting and cook for 1 hour.

2　Remove the saucepan from heat and let the mixture infuse for another hour.

3　Remove the peppers. Transfer the honey to a container, cover, and store in the refrigerator.

NOTE: Fresno and cayenne peppers produce the best results. If you're after additional heat, use habanero peppers.

YIELD: 24 COOKIES

ACTIVE TIME: 20 MINUTES

TOTAL TIME: 2 HOURS

ZESTY SHORTBREAD

4 STICKS OF UNSALTED BUTTER, AT ROOM TEMPERATURE

¼ CUP SUGAR

¼ CUP ORANGE JUICE

1 TABLESPOON ORANGE ZEST

2 TEASPOONS FINELY CHOPPED FRESH ROSEMARY

4½ CUPS ALL-PURPOSE FLOUR

CONFECTIONERS' SUGAR, TO TASTE

1 Place all of the ingredients, except for the flour and confectioners' sugar, in a mixing bowl and beat at low speed with a handheld mixer until the mixture is smooth and creamy.

2 Slowly add the flour and beat until a crumbly dough forms. Press the dough into a rectangle that is approximately ½ inch thick. Cover with plastic wrap and place the dough in the refrigerator for 1 hour.

3 Preheat the oven to 350°F and line two baking sheets with parchment paper. Cut the dough into rounds and place them on the baking sheets. Sprinkle with confectioners' sugar, place in the oven, and bake until the edges start to brown, about 15 minutes. Remove and let cool before serving.

YIELD: 16 BROWNIES

ACTIVE TIME: 15 MINUTES

TOTAL TIME: 1 HOUR AND 15 MINUTES

STOUT BROWNIES

12 OZ. GUINNESS STOUT

¾ LB. DARK
CHOCOLATE CHIPS

2 STICKS OF
UNSALTED BUTTER

1½ CUPS SUGAR

3 LARGE EGGS

1 TEASPOON PURE
VANILLA EXTRACT

¾ CUP ALL-PURPOSE FLOUR

1¼ TEASPOONS KOSHER SALT

COCOA POWDER, AS NEEDED

1 Preheat the oven to 350°F and grease a square 8-inch cake pan. Place the Guinness in a saucepan and bring to a boil. Cook until it has reduced by half. Remove pan from the heat and let cool.

2 Place the chocolate chips and the butter in a microwave-safe bowl and microwave until melted, removing to stir every 15 seconds.

3 Place the sugar, eggs, and vanilla in a large bowl and stir until combined. Slowly whisk in the chocolate-and-butter mixture and then whisk in the stout.

4 Fold in the flour and salt. Pour the batter into the greased pan, place in the oven, and bake for 35 to 40 minutes, until the surface begins to crack and a toothpick inserted in the center comes out with just a few moist crumbs attached. Remove the pan from the oven, place on a wire rack, and let cool for at least 20 minutes. When cool, sprinkle the cocoa powder over the top and cut the brownies into squares.

CHOCOLATE SOUFFLÉ

5 TABLESPOONS UNSALTED BUTTER, DIVIDED INTO TABLESPOONS AND AT ROOM TEMPERATURE

6 TABLESPOONS SUGAR

½ LB. SEMISWEET CHOCOLATE CHIPS

⅛ TEASPOON KOSHER SALT

½ TEASPOON PURE VANILLA EXTRACT

6 LARGE EGG YOLKS

8 LARGE EGG WHITES

¼ TEASPOON CREAM OF TARTAR

1   Preheat the oven to 375°F. Grease the inside of a soufflé dish with 1 tablespoon of the butter and then coat the dish with 1 tablespoon of the sugar. Place the dish in the refrigerator.

2   Place the chocolate and remaining butter in a microwave-safe bowl and microwave until melted, removing to stir every 15 seconds. Remove, stir in the salt and vanilla, and set the mixture aside.

3   Place the egg yolks and the remaining sugar in a mixing bowl and beat with a handheld mixer on medium until thick, about 3 minutes. Fold into the chocolate mixture and wipe off the beaters.

4   Place the egg whites in a mixing bowl and beat until frothy. Add the cream of tartar and beat on high until moist, stiff peaks form. Stir one-quarter of the whipped egg whites into the chocolate mixture. Gently fold the remaining egg whites into the chocolate mixture and then transfer the mixture into the soufflé dish.

5   Place in the oven and bake for about 25 minutes, until the soufflé is fully risen and set, but the interior is still creamy. Remove from the oven and serve immediately.

NOTE: Rather than one large soufflé, you can make individual ones. To do so, completely fill eight 8 oz. ramekins with the chocolate mixture and reduce the baking time to approximately 16 minutes.

YIELD: 4 SERVINGS

ACTIVE TIME: 10 MINUTES

TOTAL TIME: 2 HOURS AND 10 MINUTES

CHOCOLATE-COVERED STRAWBERRIES

2 PINTS OF STRAWBERRIES

2 CUPS SEMISWEET CHOCOLATE CHIPS

6 GRAHAM CRACKERS, CRUSHED (OPTIONAL)

½ CUP GROUND ALMONDS (OPTIONAL)

1   Wash the strawberries and pat them dry.

2   Place the chocolate chips in a microwave-safe bowl and microwave until melted, removing to stir every 15 seconds. When melted, remove from the microwave and stir until smooth.

3   Dip each strawberry into the chocolate. If desired, roll the coated strawberries in the graham cracker crumbs or the ground almonds.

4   Line a baking sheet with parchment paper and place the dipped strawberries on the sheet. Place the strawberries in the refrigerator for at least 2 hours before serving.

SUMMER

With warmth and sunshine to spare, everyone knows that summer is the time to have fun. But the incredible excitement that the long days foster has a tendency to stretch us all too thin. Centering snacks and meals around a serving board filled with the season's bounty, then, sounds like a much better time than getting sucked up in elaborate preparations and time-consuming cleanup.

One of the best things about summer is the potential for a normal, low-key gathering to stretch out into the early evening and night, powered by the momentum that good people and beautiful weather can provide. With that in mind, we've selected a series of boards and preparations that will serve as ideal launching pads for such excursions.

YIELD: 4 SERVINGS
ACTIVE TIME: 15 MINUTES
TOTAL TIME: 30 MINUTES

ZUCCHINI FRITTERS

1½ LBS. ZUCCHINI

SALT AND PEPPER, TO TASTE

¼ CUP ALL-PURPOSE FLOUR

¼ CUP GRATED
PARMESAN CHEESE

1 EGG, BEATEN

3 TABLESPOONS OLIVE OIL

1 Line a colander with cheesecloth and grate the zucchini into the colander. Generously sprinkle salt over the zucchini, stir to combine, and let sit for 1 hour. After 1 hour, press down on the zucchini to remove as much liquid from it as you can.

2 Place the zucchini, flour, Parmesan, and egg in a mixing bowl and stir to combine. Use your hands to form handfuls of the mixture into balls and then gently press down on the balls to flatten them into patties.

3 Place the oil in a cast-iron skillet and warm over medium-high heat. Working in batches, place the patties in the oil, taking care not to crowd the skillet. Cook until golden brown, about 5 minutes. Flip them over and cook for another 5 minutes, until the fritters are also golden brown on that side. Remove from the skillet, transfer to a paper towel–lined plate, and repeat with the remaining patties. When all of the fritters have been cooked, season with salt and pepper and serve.

YIELD: 16 SAMOSAS

ACTIVE TIME: 45 MINUTES

TOTAL TIME: 1 HOUR AND 30 MINUTES

SAMOSAS

FOR THE WRAPPERS

2 CUPS MAIDA FLOUR, PLUS
MORE FOR DUSTING

¼ TEASPOON KOSHER SALT

2 TABLESPOONS OLIVE OIL

½ CUP WATER, PLUS
MORE AS NEEDED

FOR THE FILLING

2 RUSSET POTATOES, PEELED
AND CHOPPED

2 TABLESPOONS VEGETABLE
OIL, PLUS MORE AS NEEDED

1 TEASPOON CORIANDER
SEEDS, CRUSHED

½ TEASPOON FENNEL
SEEDS, CRUSHED

1 PINCH FENUGREEK
SEEDS, CRUSHED

1-INCH PIECE OF FRESH
GINGER, PEELED AND MINCED

1 GARLIC CLOVE, MINCED

1 TEASPOON MINCED
JALAPEÑO PEPPER

2 TEASPOONS CHILI POWDER

Continued...

1 To begin preparations for the wrappers, place the flour and salt in a mixing bowl and use your hands to combine. Add the oil and work the mixture with your hands until it is a coarse meal. Add the water and knead the mixture until a smooth, firm dough forms. If the dough is too dry, incorporate more water, adding 1 tablespoon at a time. Cover the bowl with a kitchen towel and set aside.

2 To begin preparations for the filling, place the potatoes in a saucepan and cover with water. Bring the water to a boil and cook until fork-tender, about 20 minutes. Transfer to a bowl, mash until smooth, and set aside.

3 Place the oil in a skillet and warm over medium heat. Add the crushed seeds and cook until fragrant, about 2 minutes. Add the ginger, garlic, and jalapeño, sauté for 2 minutes, and then add the chili powder, coriander, turmeric, amchoor powder, and garam masala. Cook for another minute before adding the mashed potatoes and the curry leaves. Stir to combine, season with salt, transfer the mixture to a large mixing bowl, and let it cool completely.

4 Divide the dough for the wrappers into 8 pieces and roll each one out into a 6-inch circle on a flour-dusted work surface. Cut the circles in half and brush the flat edge of each piece with water. Fold one corner of the flat edge toward the other to make a cone and pinch to seal. Fill each cone one-third of the way with the filling, brush the opening with water, and pinch to seal. Place the sealed samosas on a parchment-lined baking sheet.

Continued...

2 TABLESPOONS CORIANDER

¾ TEASPOON TURMERIC

1 TABLESPOON
AMCHOOR POWDER

½ TEASPOON GARAM MASALA

6 CURRY LEAVES, MINCED

SALT, TO TASTE

5 Add vegetable oil to a Dutch oven until it is 3 inches deep and heat it to 325°F. Working in batches, add the filled samosas to the hot oil and fry, turning them as they cook, until they are golden brown, about 5 minutes. Transfer the cooked samosas to a paper towel–lined plate and serve once they have all been cooked.

YIELD: 4 SERVINGS

ACTIVE TIME: 10 MINUTES

TOTAL TIME: 25 MINUTES

STUFFED PEPPERS

4 YELLOW BELL PEPPERS, SEEDED AND HALVED

12 CHERRY TOMATOES, HALVED

2 GARLIC CLOVES, MINCED

2 TABLESPOONS OLIVE OIL

½ CUP CRUMBLED FETA CHEESE

1 CUP BLACK OLIVES, PITTED

SALT AND PEPPER, TO TASTE

LEAVES FROM 1 BUNCH OF FRESH BASIL

1 Preheat the oven to 375°F and place the peppers on a parchment-lined baking sheet.

2 Place the cherry tomatoes, garlic, olive oil, feta, and black olives in a mixing bowl and stir to combine. Divide the mixture between the peppers, place them in the oven, and roast until the peppers start to collapse, 10 to 15 minutes.

3 Remove the peppers from the oven and let cool slightly. Season with salt and pepper and top with the basil leaves before serving.

FETA & HERB BREAD

½ CUP FINELY CHOPPED
FRESH BASIL

½ CUP FINELY CHOPPED
FRESH CHIVES

UNSALTED BUTTER,
AS NEEDED

2 TABLESPOONS
SESAME SEEDS

1¼ CUPS ALL-PURPOSE FLOUR

1 TABLESPOON
BAKING POWDER

3 LARGE ORGANIC EGGS

¼ CUP OLIVE OIL

½ CUP PLAIN YOGURT,
PLUS 2 TABLESPOONS

½ TEASPOON SEA SALT

½ TEASPOON BLACK PEPPER

7 OZ. FETA CHEESE

1   Preheat the oven to 350°F. Combine the basil and chives in a small bowl and set aside. Grease a 9 x 5–inch loaf pan with butter and sprinkle half of the sesame seeds onto the bottom and sides, shaking the pan to coat.

2   Combine the flour and baking powder in a bowl. In a separate bowl, whisk together the eggs, oil, yogurt, salt, and pepper. Stir in the cheese and herb mixture. Fold the flour mixture into the egg mixture. Be careful not to overmix the batter, and it is okay if a few lumps remain.

3   Pour the batter into the prepared pan. Level the surface with a rubber spatula and sprinkle the remaining sesame seeds on top. Bake for 40 to 50 minutes until the top is golden and a knife inserted in the center comes out clean. Allow to cool in the pan for a few minutes and then run a knife around the pan to loosen. Transfer to a wire rack to cool completely.

YIELD: 6 PINTS
ACTIVE TIME: 20 MINUTES
TOTAL TIME: 5 TO 8 HOURS

HOT PICKLES

3 LBS. PICKLING CUCUMBERS, SLICED THIN

3 SMALL YELLOW ONIONS, SLICED THIN

1 RED BELL PEPPER, STEMMED, SEEDED, AND SLICED THIN

2 HABANERO PEPPERS, STEMMED, SEEDED, AND SLICED THIN

3 GARLIC CLOVES, SLICED

3 CUPS SUGAR

3 CUPS APPLE CIDER VINEGAR

2 TABLESPOONS MUSTARD SEEDS

2 TEASPOONS TURMERIC

1 TEASPOON BLACK PEPPERCORNS

⅓ CUP CANNING AND PICKLING SALT

1   Place the cucumbers, onions, peppers, and garlic in a large bowl.

2   Place the sugar, apple cider vinegar, mustard seeds, turmeric, and peppercorns in a large pot and bring to a boil over medium-high heat, stirring to dissolve the sugar.

3   Add the vegetables and the salt and return to a boil. Remove the pot from heat and let it cool slightly.

4   To can these pickles, see page 38. If you are not interested in canning them, let cool completely before storing in the refrigerator. They will keep in the refrigerator for up to 2 weeks.

PEPPER MAYONNAISE

Place 1 cup mayonnaise, 3 tablespoons grated Parmesan cheese, 1 tablespoon lemon zest, 3 tablespoons fresh lemon juice, 1½ teaspoons black pepper, and 2 teaspoons kosher salt in a mixing bowl and whisk until combined.

YIELD: 4 SERVINGS

ACTIVE TIME: 20 MINUTES

TOTAL TIME: 30 MINUTES

PAN-FRIED ARTICHOKES

2 LARGE ARTICHOKES

1 LEMON, QUARTERED

VEGETABLE OIL, AS NEEDED

SALT, TO TASTE

LEMON-PEPPER MAYONNAISE
(SEE SIDEBAR), FOR SERVING

1 Prepare the artichokes by using a serrated knife to cut off the top half with the leaves and all but the last inch of the stem; continue whittling away the outer leaves until you see the hairy-looking choke within.

2 Using a paring knife, peel away the outer layer of the remaining part of the stem; cut the remaining artichoke into quarters and remove the hairy part in the middle. You should have the heart with a little bit of lower leaves left. Place in a bowl of water, add a squeeze of lemon juice, and set aside.

3 Bring water to a boil in a small saucepan. Add the artichokes and parboil until they begin to feel tender, about 3 to 5 minutes. Remove from the water and drain.

4 Place another small pot on the stove and fill with enough oil that the artichoke hearts will be submerged. Warm the oil over medium heat until it starts to sizzle.

5 Place the artichokes in the oil and fry until they are brown all over, turning occasionally, 8 to 10 minutes. Transfer to a paper towel–lined plate to drain and let cool. Sprinkle with salt and serve with the lemon wedges and the Lemon-Pepper Mayonnaise.

YIELD: 4 SERVINGS

ACTIVE TIME: 10 MINUTES

TOTAL TIME: 30 MINUTES

KALE CHIPS

1 BUNCH OF KALE,
STEMS REMOVED

1 TEASPOON KOSHER SALT

½ TEASPOON BLACK PEPPER

½ TEASPOON PAPRIKA

½ TEASPOON DRIED PARSLEY

½ TEASPOON DRIED BASIL

¼ TEASPOON DRIED THYME

¼ TEASPOON DRIED SAGE

2 TABLESPOONS OLIVE OIL

1   Preheat the oven to 350°F. Tear the kale leaves into smaller pieces and place them in a mixing bowl. Add the remaining ingredients and work the mixture with your hands until the kale is evenly coated.

2   Divide the seasoned kale between 2 parchment-lined baking sheets so that it sits on each in an even layer. Place in the oven and bake until crispy, 6 to 8 minutes. Remove and let cool before serving.

YIELD: 8 SERVINGS

ACTIVE TIME: 30 MINUTES

TOTAL TIME: 1 HOUR AND 30 MINUTES

DILL PICKLE ARANCINI

8 CUPS CHICKEN STOCK

1 STICK OF UNSALTED BUTTER

2 CUPS ARBORIO RICE

1 SMALL WHITE ONION, MINCED

1 CUP WHITE WINE

1½ CUPS HAVARTI CHEESE WITH DILL, GRATED

1½ CUPS CHOPPED DILL PICKLES

SALT AND BLACK PEPPER, TO TASTE

4 CUPS VEGETABLE OIL

6 LARGE EGGS, BEATEN

5 CUPS PANKO

1   Bring the chicken stock to a simmer in a large saucepan. In a skillet, melt the butter over high heat. Once the butter is foaming, add the rice and onion and cook until the onion is translucent, about 4 minutes. Deglaze the skillet with the white wine and cook until the wine has almost completely evaporated. Then, reduce the heat to medium-high and begin adding the hot chicken stock ¼ cup at a time, stirring until it has been incorporated. Continue this process until all of the stock has been incorporated and the rice is tender.

2   Turn off the heat, add the cheese and pickles, and season with salt and pepper. Pour the mixture onto a baking sheet and let cool.

3   Place the oil in a Dutch oven and warm over medium heat until it reaches 350°F. When the rice mixture is cool, form it into golf ball–sized spheres. Dip them into the eggs and then dip them into the panko until coated all over. Place the balls in the oil and cook until warmed through and golden brown. Drain on a paper towel–lined plate and let cool before serving.

YIELD: 4 SERVINGS

ACTIVE TIME: 30 MINUTES

TOTAL TIME: 1 HOUR AND 45 MINUTES

PORK EMPANADAS

FOR THE DOUGH

¼ TEASPOON KOSHER SALT

6 TABLESPOONS WARM
WATER (110°F)

1½ CUPS ALL-PURPOSE FLOUR,
PLUS MORE AS NEEDED

3 TABLESPOONS LARD
OR UNSALTED BUTTER, CUT
INTO SMALL PIECES

FOR THE FILLING

2 TEASPOONS OLIVE OIL,
PLUS MORE AS NEEDED

1 YELLOW ONION, MINCED

1 GARLIC CLOVE, MINCED

¾ LB. GROUND PORK

1 (14 OZ.) CAN OF CRUSHED
TOMATOES

½ TEASPOON KOSHER SALT

¼ TEASPOON BLACK PEPPER

Continued...

1   To prepare the dough, dissolve the salt in the warm water. Place the flour in a mixing bowl, add the lard or butter, and work the mixture with a pastry blender until it is coarse crumbs. Add the salted water and knead the mixture until a stiff dough forms. Cut the dough into eight pieces, cover them with plastic wrap, and chill in the refrigerator for 20 minutes.

2   To prepare the filling, place the olive oil in a skillet and warm over medium heat. When the oil starts to shimmer, add the onion and cook until it has softened, about 5 minutes. Add the garlic, cook for 2 minutes, and then add the ground pork. Cook, while breaking it up with a fork, until light brown, about 5 minutes. Drain off any excess fat and add the tomatoes, salt, pepper, cinnamon stick, cloves, raisins, and vinegar. Simmer until the filling is thick, about 30 minutes. Remove from heat and let cool before folding in the toasted almonds.

3   Add olive oil to a Dutch oven until it is 2 inches deep and bring it to 350°F. Preheat the oven to 200°F and place a platter in the oven. Place the pieces of dough on a flour-dusted work surface and roll each one into a 5-inch circle. Place 3 tablespoons of the filling in the center of one circle, brush the edge with water, and fold into a half-moon. Press down on the edge to seal the empanada tight, trying to remove as much air as possible. Repeat with the remaining filling and pieces of dough.

Continued...

1 CINNAMON STICK,
FINELY CHOPPED

2 WHOLE CLOVES

2 TABLESPOONS RAISINS

2 TEASPOONS APPLE
CIDER VINEGAR

2 TABLESPOONS SLIVERED
ALMONDS, TOASTED

4 Working in two batches, place the empanadas in the hot oil and fry until golden brown, about 5 minutes. Drain the cooked empanadas on paper towels and place them in the warm oven while you cook the next batch.

YIELD: 8 SERVINGS

ACTIVE TIME: 15 MINUTES

TOTAL TIME: 1 HOUR AND 40 MINUTES

SALMON & DILL QUICHE

1 TEASPOON DIJON MUSTARD

1 PIECRUST, BLIND BAKED
(SEE PAGE 37)

1 LB. SMOKED SALMON, TORN
INTO BITE-SIZED PIECES

4 EGGS

1 CUP HALF-AND-HALF

1 TEASPOON KOSHER SALT

½ TEASPOON BLACK PEPPER

1 TABLESPOON FINELY
CHOPPED FRESH DILL

½ CUP CREAM CHEESE, AT
ROOM TEMPERATURE

1 Preheat the oven to 350°F. Brush the mustard over the bottom of the piecrust. Distribute the salmon pieces over the crust and set it aside.

2 Place the eggs, half-and-half, salt, and pepper in a mixing bowl and stir until combined. Stir in the dill, pour the egg mixture over the salmon, and shake the pie plate to evenly distribute the liquid.

3 Dot the mixture with spoonfuls of the cream cheese, place the quiche in the oven, and bake for about 35 minutes, until it is puffy and golden brown. Remove from the oven and let cool for 10 minutes before serving.

CORNBREAD

5 EARS OF CORN, SILK REMOVED

10 TABLESPOONS UNSALTED BUTTER

1 CUP DICED ONION

3 GARLIC CLOVES, MINCED

2 TEASPOONS KOSHER SALT, PLUS MORE TO TASTE

2¾ CUPS HEAVY CREAM

2 CUPS ALL-PURPOSE FLOUR

2 CUPS CORNMEAL

¼ CUP GENTLY PACKED BROWN SUGAR

2 TABLESPOONS BAKING POWDER

½ TEASPOON CAYENNE PEPPER

½ TEASPOON PAPRIKA

1½ CUPS HONEY

6 EGGS

¼ CUP SOUR CREAM

1   Preheat the oven to 400°F.

2   Place the ears of corn on a baking sheet, place it in the oven, and bake for 25 minutes, until the kernels have a slight give to them. Remove from the oven and let cool. When the ears of corn are cool enough to handle, remove the husks and cut the kernels from the cob. Lower the oven temperature to 300°F.

3   Place 2 tablespoons of the butter in a large saucepan and melt over medium heat. Add the onion and garlic, season with salt, and cook until the onion is translucent. Set ¾ cup of the corn kernels aside and add the rest to the pan. Add 2 cups of the cream and a pinch of salt and cook until the corn is very tender, about 15 to 20 minutes.

4   Strain, reserve the cream, and transfer the solids to the blender. Puree until smooth, adding the cream as needed if the mixture is too thick. Season to taste and allow the puree to cool completely.

5   Place the flour, cornmeal, salt, brown sugar, baking powder, cayenne pepper, and paprika in a large mixing bowl and stir until combined. Place 2 cups of the corn puree, the honey, eggs, remaining cream, and sour cream in a separate large mixing bowl and stir until combined. Gradually add the dry mixture to the wet mixture and stir to combine. When all of the wet mixture has been incorporated, add the reserved corn kernels and fold the mixture until they are evenly distributed.

Continued...

6　Grease an 11 x 7–inch baking pan and pour the batter into it. Place the pan in the oven and bake until a toothpick inserted into the center comes out clean, about 35 minutes. Remove from the oven and briefly cool before cutting.

YIELD: 5 PINTS

ACTIVE TIME: 10 MINUTES

TOTAL TIME: 1 WEEK

DILLY BEANS

3 LBS. GREEN BEANS

2½ CUPS WHITE VINEGAR

2½ CUPS WATER

¼ CUP PICKLING SALT

5 GARLIC CLOVES

5 TEASPOONS DILL SEEDS
(NOT DILL WEED)

5 TEASPOONS RED
PEPPER FLAKES

1 Wash and trim the beans so that they will fit in the jars. If the beans are particularly long, cut them in half. Place the vinegar, water, and salt in a medium saucepan and bring to a boil.

2 While the brine heats up, pack your beans into mason jars, leaving ½ inch of space free at the top.

3 Divide the garlic cloves, dill seeds, and red pepper flakes evenly between the jars.

4 Slowly pour the hot brine over the beans, leaving ½ inch free at the top. To can these beans, see page 38. If you are not interested in canning them, let cool completely before storing in the refrigerator, where they will keep for up to 2 weeks.

YIELD: 8 CUPS

ACTIVE TIME: 20 MINUTES

TOTAL TIME: 1 HOUR AND 30 MINUTES

APRICOT & CHILI JAM

2 LBS. APRICOTS, HALVED, PITTED, AND CHOPPED

ZEST AND JUICE OF 1 LEMON

2 LBS. SUGAR

1 CUP WATER

3 RED CHILI PEPPERS, SEEDED AND MINCED

1 TABLESPOON UNSALTED BUTTER

1 Place all of the ingredients, other than the butter, in a saucepan and bring to a gentle boil over medium heat, while stirring to help the sugar dissolve. Boil for about 5 minutes.

2 Reduce the heat and simmer for 15 minutes, stirring frequently. If you prefer a smoother jam, mash the mixture with a wooden spoon as it cooks.

3 When the jam has started to form a thin skin, remove the pan from the heat. Add the butter and stir to disperse any froth. Remove and let cool for 15 minutes. To can this jam, see page 38. If you are not interested in canning it, let the jam cool completely before storing in the refrigerator.

YIELD: 2 CUPS

ACTIVE TIME: 35 MINUTES

TOTAL TIME: 5 TO 7 HOURS

GREEN TOMATO JAM

¾ LB. GREEN TOMATOES, DICED

¼ LARGE ONION, DICED

½-INCH PIECE OF FRESH GINGER, PEELED AND MINCED

2 GARLIC CLOVES, CHOPPED

1 TEASPOON MUSTARD SEEDS

1 TEASPOON CUMIN

1 TEASPOON CORIANDER

2 TEASPOONS KOSHER SALT

½ CUP HONEY OR MAPLE SYRUP

1 CUP APPLE CIDER VINEGAR

1 CUP RAISINS

1 Place all of the ingredients in a large saucepan and bring to a boil. Reduce to a simmer and cook, stirring occasionally, until the onion and tomatoes are tender and the juices have thickened, 20 to 30 minutes. If a smoother jam is desired, mash the mixture with a wooden spoon as it simmers.

2 Remove the jam from heat and let cool for 15 minutes. To can this jam, see page 38. If you are not interested in canning it, let cool completely before storing in the refrigerator.

YIELD: ½ CUP
ACTIVE TIME: 10 MINUTES
TOTAL TIME: 10 MINUTES

HERB BUTTER

1 TABLESPOON OLIVE OIL

1 GARLIC CLOVE

1 TABLESPOON FINELY
CHOPPED FRESH THYME

1 TABLESPOON FINELY
CHOPPED FRESH BASIL

1 STICK OF UNSALTED BUTTER

1 Place the olive oil and garlic in a food processor and puree until the garlic is minced. Add the thyme and basil and puree until incorporated. Set aside.

2 Place the butter in a mixing bowl and beat with a handheld mixer at medium speed until it is pale and fluffy.

3 Add the infused oil to the butter and beat until incorporated.

4 Serve the butter immediately, or store it in the refrigerator until ready to serve.

YIELD: ½ CUP
ACTIVE TIME: 2 MINUTES
TOTAL TIME: 2 MINUTES

SPICY HONEY MUSTARD DIP

½ CUP MAYONNAISE

2 TABLESPOONS
DIJON MUSTARD

2 TABLESPOONS HOT HONEY
(SEE PAGE 59)

1 TABLESPOON FRESH
LEMON JUICE

SALT, TO TASTE

1 Place all of the ingredients in a mixing bowl and stir until combined. Serve immediately.

YIELD: 6 CUPS

ACTIVE TIME: 5 MINUTES

TOTAL TIME: 5 MINUTES

HEAVENLY CRUDITÉ DIP

1½ CUPS MAYONNAISE

2 CUPS SOUR CREAM

1 TABLESPOON FINELY
CHOPPED FRESH PARSLEY

1 TABLESPOON FINELY
CHOPPED FRESH TARRAGON

1 TABLESPOON FINELY
CHOPPED FRESH CHIVES

1 TABLESPOON FINELY
CHOPPED FRESH BASIL

1 TABLESPOON RED
WINE VINEGAR

1 TABLESPOON SUGAR

1 TEASPOON GARLIC POWDER

1 TABLESPOON
WORCESTERSHIRE SAUCE

SALT AND PEPPER, TO TASTE

6 OZ. BLUE CHEESE

1   Place all of the ingredients, except for the blue cheese, in a food processor and puree until smooth.

2   Add the blue cheese and pulse a few times, making sure to maintain a chunky texture. Serve or store in the refrigerator.

TOMATO CONCASSE

Concasse, French for "to crush or grind," refers to tomatoes that have been peeled, seeded, and then chopped. To do this easily, boil enough water for a tomato to be submerged and add a pinch of salt. Prepare an ice water bath and score the top of the tomato with a paring knife. Place the tomato in the boiling water for 30 seconds, carefully remove it, and place it in the ice water bath. Once the tomato is cool, remove from the water and peel with the paring knife. Cut into quarters, remove the seeds, and chop.

YIELD: 2 CUPS
ACTIVE TIME: 5 MINUTES
TOTAL TIME: 5 MINUTES

GUACAMOLE

2 TABLESPOONS MINCED
RED ONION

ZEST AND JUICE OF 1 LIME

SALT, TO TASTE

1 JALAPEÑO PEPPER,
STEMMED, SEEDED,
AND MINCED

FLESH OF 3 AVOCADOS,
CHOPPED

2 TABLESPOONS FINELY
CHOPPED FRESH CILANTRO

1 PLUM TOMATO, CONCASSE
(SEE SIDEBAR)

1   Place the onion, lime zest and juice, salt, and jalapeño in a mixing bowl and stir to combine.

2   Add the avocados and work the mixture with a fork until the desired consistency has been reached. Add the cilantro and tomato, stir to incorporate, and taste. Adjust seasoning if necessary and serve immediately.

YIELD: 6 SERVINGS

ACTIVE TIME: 20 MINUTES

TOTAL TIME: 1 HOUR AND 45 MINUTES

CHEESE DIP

1 CUP CREAM CHEESE OR QUARK CHEESE, AT ROOM TEMPERATURE

½ CUP SOUR CREAM

1 CUP SHREDDED MOZZARELLA CHEESE, PLUS MORE AS NEEDED

2 TABLESPOONS FRESH ROSEMARY LEAVES

2 TABLESPOONS FRESH THYME LEAVES

½ CUP DICED SUMMER SQUASH

1 CUP SWISS CHARD

1 CUP SPINACH

6 GARLIC CLOVES, DICED

2 TEASPOONS KOSHER SALT

1 TEASPOON BLACK PEPPER

SLICES OF CRUSTY BREAD, FOR SERVING

1 Place the cheese, sour cream, and mozzarella in an oven-safe bowl and stir until well combined.

2 Add the remaining ingredients for the dip, stir to combine, and place in the refrigerator for at least 1 hour.

3 Approximately 30 minutes before you are ready to serve the dip, preheat the oven to 350°F. Top the dip with additional mozzarella and bake until the cheese is melted and slightly brown, about 20 minutes. Remove from the oven and let cool briefly before serving.

NOTE: Quark is a creamy, unripe cheese that is popular in Germany and Eastern European countries. If you're intrigued, Vermont Creamery produces a widely available version.

YIELD: 4 CUPS

ACTIVE TIME: 30 MINUTES

TOTAL TIME: 3 TO 7 DAYS

KIMCHI

1 NAPA CABBAGE, CUT INTO STRIPS

½ CUP KOSHER SALT

2-INCH PIECE OF FRESH GINGER, PEELED AND MINCED

3 GARLIC CLOVES, MINCED

1 TEASPOON SUGAR

5 TABLESPOONS RED PEPPER FLAKES

3 BUNCHES OF SCALLIONS, TRIMMED AND SLICED

WATER, AS NEEDED

1 Place the cabbage and salt in a large bowl and stir to combine. Wash your hands, or put on gloves, and work the mixture with your hands, squeezing to remove as much liquid as possible from the cabbage. Let the mixture rest for 2 hours.

2 Add the remaining ingredients, except for the water, work the mixture with your hands until well combined, and squeeze to remove as much liquid as possible.

3 Transfer the mixture to a large mason jar and press down so it is tightly packed together. The liquid should be covering the mixture. If it is not, add water until the mixture is covered.

4 Cover the jar and let the mixture sit at room temperature for 3 to 7 days, removing the lid daily to release the gas that has built up.

YIELD: 2 CUPS

ACTIVE TIME: 5 MINUTES

TOTAL TIME: 1 HOUR

TZATZIKI

1 CUP PLAIN FULL-
FAT YOGURT

¾ CUP SEEDED AND
MINCED CUCUMBER

1 GARLIC CLOVE, MINCED

JUICE FROM 1 LEMON WEDGE

SALT AND WHITE PEPPER,
TO TASTE

FRESH PARSLEY OR DILL,
FINELY CHOPPED, TO TASTE

1 Place the yogurt, cucumber, garlic, and lemon juice in a mixing bowl and stir to combine. Taste and add salt and pepper as needed. Stir in the parsley or dill.

2 Place in the refrigerator and chill for about an hour before serving.

YIELD: 2 CUPS

ACTIVE TIME: 10 MINUTES

TOTAL TIME: 10 MINUTES

CREAM CHEESE & RADISH DIP

2 CUPS RADISHES

½ CUP CREAM CHEESE, AT ROOM TEMPERATURE

⅓ CUP SOUR CREAM

2 TABLESPOONS FINELY CHOPPED FRESH CHIVES

SALT AND PEPPER, TO TASTE

HOT SAUCE, TO TASTE

1　Roughly chop the radishes to the desired chunkiness of the dip and set aside.

2　Place the cream cheese and sour cream in a bowl and stir until smooth.

3　Fold in the chives and radishes and season with salt, pepper, and hot sauce.

YIELD: 1 CUP

ACTIVE TIME: 20 MINUTES

TOTAL TIME: 2 HOURS

SALSA

1 LB. RIPE TOMATOES, CORED
AND HALVED

1½ TEASPOONS OLIVE OIL

SALT AND PEPPER, TO TASTE

2 TABLESPOONS MINCED
YELLOW ONION

½ JALAPEÑO PEPPER,
STEMMED, SEEDED,
AND MINCED

1 TABLESPOON FINELY
CHOPPED FRESH CILANTRO

1 TABLESPOON FRESH
LIME JUICE

1   Preheat your oven to 450°F. Place the tomatoes, olive oil, salt, and
pepper in a large bowl and toss to coat. Let stand for 30 minutes.

2   Place the tomatoes, cut-side down, on a baking sheet, place them
in the oven, and roast until they start to char and soften, about
10 minutes. Carefully turn the tomatoes over and cook until they
start bubbling, about 5 minutes. Remove from the oven and let the
tomatoes cool completely.

3   Chop the tomatoes and place them in a bowl with the remaining
ingredients. Stir to combine and let stand at room temperature for
45 minutes. Taste, adjust the seasoning if necessary, and serve.
The salsa will keep in the refrigerator for up to 2 days.

YIELD: 3½ CUPS

ACTIVE TIME: 10 MINUTES

TOTAL TIME: 1 HOUR AND 30 MINUTES

BLUEBERRY & BASIL JAM

3 QUARTS OF BLUEBERRIES

LEAVES FROM 1 BUNCH OF BASIL, FINELY CHOPPED

2 TEASPOONS FRESH LEMON JUICE

2 CUPS SUGAR

½ CUP WATER

1   Place all of the ingredients in a large saucepan and bring to a boil, while stirring frequently, over medium-high heat.

2   Once the mixture has come to a boil, reduce the heat so that it simmers and cook, while stirring frequently, until the mixture has reduced by half and is starting to thicken, about 1 hour. Remove from heat and let it thicken and set as it cools. If the jam is still too thin after 1 hour, continue to simmer until it is the desired consistency.

3   To can this jam, see page 38. If you are not interested in canning it, let cool completely before storing in the refrigerator, where it will keep for up to 1 week.

YIELD: 2½ CUPS

ACTIVE TIME: 10 MINUTES

TOTAL TIME: 1 HOUR AND 30 MINUTES

MIXED BERRY JAM

3 PINTS OF STRAWBERRIES, HULLED, CORED, AND QUARTERED

1 PINT OF BLUEBERRIES

1 PINT OF RASPBERRIES

½ CUP SUGAR

1¼ TABLESPOONS PECTIN

1   Place the berries and sugar in a large saucepan and cook, while stirring, over medium-high heat. When the sugar has dissolved and the berries start breaking down and releasing their liquid, reduce the heat to medium and cook, while stirring every 10 minutes, until the berries are very soft and the mixture has thickened, 30 to 40 minutes.

2   While stirring, sprinkle the pectin onto the mixture and cook for another minute. To can this jam, see page 38. If you are not interested in canning it, let cool completely before storing in the refrigerator, where it will keep for up to 1 week.

YIELD: 8 SERVINGS

ACTIVE TIME: 40 MINUTES

TOTAL TIME: 2 HOURS

SWEET STRAWBERRY POCKETS

3 QUARTS OF FRESH STRAWBERRIES, HULLED AND SLICED

1 CUP GRANULATED SUGAR

2 TEASPOONS FRESH LEMON JUICE

1 TABLESPOON CORNSTARCH

1½ TEASPOONS WATER

1 PIECRUST

2 EGGS, BEATEN

1½ CUPS SIFTED CONFECTIONERS' SUGAR

3 TABLESPOONS WHOLE MILK

1 TEASPOON CINNAMON

1   Preheat the oven to 400°F. Place the strawberries on a baking sheet and roast in the oven until they start to darken and release their juice, about 20 to 30 minutes. If you prefer, you can roast them for up to an hour. Cooking the strawberries for longer will caramelize the sugars and lend them an even richer flavor.

2   Remove the strawberries from the oven and place them in a saucepan with the sugar and lemon juice. Bring to a simmer over medium heat and cook for 20 minutes, until the mixture has thickened slightly.

3   Place the cornstarch and water in a small cup and stir until there are no lumps in the mixture. Add the slurry to the saucepan and stir until the mixture is viscous. Remove from heat.

4   Roll out the piecrust, divide it into two squares, and then cut each square into quarters. Spoon some of the strawberry mixture into the center of each quarter.

Continued...

5 Take a bottom corner of each pie and fold to the opposite top corner. Press down to ensure that none of the mixture leaks out and then use a fork to crimp the edge and seal. Place the handpies on a baking sheet and brush them with the beaten eggs. Place in the oven and bake until golden brown, about 20 to 30 minutes.

6 While the pies are cooking, place the confectioners' sugar, milk, and cinnamon in a bowl and stir until well combined.

7 Remove the pies from the oven, brush them with the sugar-and-cinnamon glaze, and let cool before serving.

BLUEBERRY BUCKLE

2 CUPS ALL-PURPOSE FLOUR

¾ CUP GRANULATED SUGAR

½ CUP PACKED LIGHT BROWN SUGAR

¼ TEASPOON CINNAMON

¾ TEASPOON KOSHER SALT

14 TABLESPOONS UNSALTED BUTTER, CUT INTO SMALL PIECES AND AT ROOM TEMPERATURE

1½ TEASPOONS BAKING POWDER

½ TEASPOON LEMON ZEST

1½ TEASPOONS PURE VANILLA EXTRACT

2 LARGE EGGS, AT ROOM TEMPERATURE

1 QUART OF BLUEBERRIES

1   Preheat the oven to 350°F and grease a cake pan with nonstick cooking spray.

2   Place ½ cup of the flour, 2 tablespoons of the granulated sugar, the brown sugar, cinnamon, and a pinch of the salt in a mixing bowl and stir until combined. Add 4 tablespoons of the butter and work the mixture with a pastry blender until it resembles wet sand. Set aside.

3   Place the remaining flour and the baking powder in a small bowl and whisk to combine. Place the remaining butter, sugar, salt, and the lemon zest in a separate mixing bowl and beat until the mixture is light and fluffy. Add the vanilla, beat until incorporated, and then add the eggs one at a time. Beat until incorporated and then gradually add the flour mixture. Beat until all of the flour has been incorporated. Add the blueberries and then fold the batter until it is homogenous and the blueberries have been evenly distributed. Scrape down the bowl as needed while mixing the batter.

4   Transfer the batter to the cake pan and smooth the surface with a rubber spatula. Sprinkle the sugar-and-cinnamon mixture over the batter, place the cake in the oven, and bake until the top is golden brown and a toothpick inserted into the center comes out clean, about 50 minutes. Remove from the oven and let cool in the pan for 15 minutes.

5   Remove from the pan, transfer to a wire rack, and let cool to room temperature before serving.

YIELD: 6 TO 8 SERVINGS

ACTIVE TIME: 15 MINUTES

TOTAL TIME: 45 MINUTES

PEACH GALETTE

1 PIECRUST

ALL-PURPOSE FLOUR, AS NEEDED

3 CUPS PEELED AND SLICED PEACHES

½ CUP SUGAR, PLUS 1 TABLESPOON

JUICE OF ½ LEMON

3 TABLESPOONS CORNSTARCH

PINCH OF KOSHER SALT

1 TEASPOON AMARETTO LIQUEUR (OPTIONAL)

2 TABLESPOONS PEACH JAM

1 EGG, BEATEN

1　Preheat the oven to 400°F. Place the piecrust on a flour-dusted work surface, roll it out into a 9-inch circle, and place the dough on a parchment-lined baking sheet.

2　Place the peaches, ½ cup sugar, lemon juice, cornstarch, and salt in a mixing bowl and stir until the peaches are evenly coated.

3　If using the Amaretto, place it in a bowl, add the jam, and stir to combine. Spread the jam mixture (or just the jam) over the dough, making sure to leave 1½ inches of dough uncovered at the edge. Spread the filling over the jam and fold the uncovered dough over the filling.

4　Brush the crust with the egg and sprinkle the remaining sugar over it. Place the galette in the oven and bake until the crust is golden brown and the filling is bubbling, about 35 minutes. Remove from the oven and let cool before serving.

YIELD: 12 TARTS
ACTIVE TIME: 35 MINUTES
TOTAL TIME: 2 HOURS

MINIATURE RASPBERRY TARTS

1 PIECRUST

ALL-PURPOSE FLOUR, AS NEEDED

2¾ CUPS WHOLE MILK

⅛ TEASPOON KOSHER SALT

⅔ CUP GRANULATED SUGAR

4 EGG YOLKS

¼ CUP CORNSTARCH

2 TABLESPOONS UNSALTED BUTTER

1 TEASPOON PURE VANILLA EXTRACT

1 CUP FRESH RASPBERRIES

CONFECTIONERS' SUGAR, AS NEEDED

1 Preheat the oven to 350°F and spray a muffin tin with nonstick cooking spray.

2 Roll out the piecrust on a flour-dusted work surface to ¼ inch thick. Using a floured biscuit cutter or mason jar, cut 12 rounds out of the dough and place them in the wells of the muffin tin. Place in the oven and bake until golden brown, about 25 minutes. Remove from the oven and let cool.

3 Place the milk, salt, and sugar in large saucepan and bring to a simmer over medium heat.

4 Place the egg yolks and cornstarch in a large bowl and whisk to combine. While whisking constantly, add the warm milk mixture to the egg mixture in ½-cup increments. When 2 cups of the milk mixture have been incorporated, add the tempered eggs to the saucepan, while whisking constantly to incorporate.

5 Cook the mixture over medium-low heat, while stirring constantly, until it starts to thicken. Stir in the butter and vanilla and spoon the mixture into the baked tart shells. Place in the refrigerator and chill until cool.

6 Remove from the refrigerator, top each tart with a few raspberries and a dusting of confectioners' sugar, and serve.

FALL

Fall is a time to slow down and reflect on the good times had in the recent past and the celebrations to come. Since there is a greater tendency to take it easy when autumn arrives, and the crisp air and vibrant leaves frame each day in splendor, it is perhaps the best season for the serving board.

The sun is still warm enough that light, vegetable-based spreads and dips feel of the moment, but the crisp air elicits a desire for more substantial, heartier preparations. We've got a generous offering of each, so break out those platters, and recognize that nearly anything you could think to put on them will suit the season, and the occasion.

YIELD: 6 SERVINGS
ACTIVE TIME: 10 MINUTES
TOTAL TIME: 10 MINUTES

CRISPY WONTON SKINS

OLIVE OIL, AS NEEDED

4 WONTON WRAPPERS,
CUT INTO TRIANGLES

SALT, TO TASTE

1 Add olive oil to a Dutch oven until it is about 1 inch deep and warm to 350°F over medium-high heat.

2 Add the wonton wrappers and fry, while turning frequently, until they are crisp and golden brown, about 3 minutes. Place the wrappers on a paper towel–lined plate to drain, season with salt, and serve.

YIELD: 12 SERVINGS
ACTIVE TIME: 15 MINUTES
TOTAL TIME: 30 MINUTES

CHEESE STRAWS

2 SHEETS OF FROZEN PUFF
PASTRY, THAWED

ALL-PURPOSE FLOUR,
AS NEEDED

½ CUP GRATED
FONTINA CHEESE

½ CUP GRATED
PARMESAN CHEESE

1 TEASPOON FINELY CHOPPED
FRESH THYME

1 TEASPOON BLACK PEPPER

1 EGG, BEATEN

1 Preheat the oven to 375°F and line a baking sheet with parchment paper. Place the sheets of puff pastry on a flour-dusted surface and roll out until the sheets are approximately 10 x 12–inch rectangles.

2 Place the cheeses, thyme, and pepper in a mixing bowl and stir to combine.

3 Lightly brush the tops of the pastry sheets with the egg. Sprinkle the cheese mixture over them and gently press down so it adheres to the pastry.

4 Cut the sheets into ¼-inch-wide strips and twist them. Place the twists on the baking sheet, place in the oven, and bake for 12 to 15 minutes, until twists are golden brown and puffy. Turn the twists over and bake for another 2 to 3 minutes.

5 Remove from the oven and let the twists cool on a wire rack before serving.

YIELD: 6 SERVINGS

ACTIVE TIME: 1 HOUR

TOTAL TIME: 1 HOUR AND 45 MINUTES

PORK POT STICKERS

1 TEASPOON
CORIANDER SEEDS

8 WHOLE CLOVES

½ TEASPOON SICHUAN
PEPPERCORNS

½ TEASPOON BLACK
PEPPERCORNS

1 STAR ANISE POD

2 CARDAMOM PODS, CRUSHED

2 BAY LEAVES

2 CINNAMON STICKS,
BROKEN INTO BITS

2½ LBS. BUTTERNUT SQUASH,
PEELED, SEEDED, AND CUBED

2 TABLESPOONS OLIVE OIL

½ LB. GROUND PORK

3 TABLESPOONS
MINCED GINGER

Continued...

1   Place all of the spices in a small skillet over medium heat and toast, stirring constantly, until fragrant, about 2 minutes. Transfer to a spice grinder or food processor and grind into a fine powder.

2   Preheat the oven to 350°F. Toss the squash with the oil and 1 tablespoon of the toasted spice mixture. Place on a parchment-lined baking sheet, place it in the oven, and roast, turning the squash over after about 15 minutes, until lightly caramelized and soft, about 30 minutes.

3   While the squash is cooking, add the ground pork to the skillet and cook over medium heat until cooked through, about 10 minutes.

4   Remove the squash from the oven, place it in a large bowl, and mash with a fork until smooth. Add the pork, ginger, rice wine, soy sauce, sesame oil, three of the scallions, the egg white, and 1 tablespoon of the toasted spice mixture and stir until thoroughly combined.

5   Line a baking sheet with parchment paper and prepare a small bowl of water for sealing.

Continued...

3 TABLESPOONS SHAOXING
RICE WINE OR DRY SHERRY

5 TABLESPOONS SOY SAUCE

1 TABLESPOON TOASTED
SESAME OIL

5 SCALLIONS, TRIMMED
AND MINCED

1 EGG WHITE,
LIGHTLY BEATEN

30 DUMPLING WRAPPERS

2 TABLESPOONS PEANUT OIL

WATER, AS NEEDED

6 Place a wrapper in front of you and place a heaping teaspoon of filling in the middle of it. Dip your finger in the water and run it along the edges of the wrapper. Fold one of the corners over the filling to create a triangle and press down the edges together to seal, pushing down to remove as much air as you can. Repeat with the remaining wrappers and filling.

7 Place 1 tablespoon of the peanut oil in a large skillet and warm over medium-high heat. When it starts to shimmer, add the dumplings in batches and cook until they are golden brown on the bottom. Add 2 tablespoons water, cover, and steam until cooked through, about 4 minutes. Transfer the cooked dumplings to a warmed platter and tent with foil to keep warm. Dry the skillet with a paper towel and repeat until all of the pot stickers have been cooked. Sprinkle the remaining scallions over them and serve immediately.

YIELD: 8 PRETZELS

ACTIVE TIME: 20 MINUTES

TOTAL TIME: 1 HOUR AND 20 MINUTES

PRETZELS

2¼ TEASPOONS
INSTANT YEAST

1½ CUPS LUKEWARM
WATER (90°F)

1 TEASPOON SUGAR

2½ CUPS ALL-PURPOSE FLOUR

½ TEASPOON SEA SALT, PLUS
MORE TO TASTE

1 TABLESPOON BAKING SODA

OLIVE OIL, AS NEEDED

3 TABLESPOONS UNSALTED
BUTTER, MELTED

1 Place the yeast, 1 cup of the water, and sugar in a mixing bowl and let the mixture sit for 10 minutes.

2 Stir in the flour and salt and work the mixture until it just holds together. Knead the dough until it is soft and smooth. Cover the bowl with a kitchen towel and let it sit for 30 minutes.

3 Preheat the oven to 450°F and grease a baking sheet with olive oil. Place the dough on a piece of waxed paper and cut it into eight pieces.

4 Place the water and baking soda in a small bowl, stir to combine, and microwave for 1 minute. Roll each of the eight pieces into a long rope, then shape them into pretzels. Dip each pretzel into the baking soda-and-water mixture and place on the baking sheet. Sprinkle salt over the top and let them rest for 10 minutes.

5 Place the pretzels in the oven and bake for about 10 minutes, until they are golden brown. Remove from the oven, brush the pretzels with the melted butter, and serve warm.

YIELD: 2 CUPS
ACTIVE TIME: 15 MINUTES
TOTAL TIME: 45 MINUTES

SWEET WALNUTS

1 TABLESPOON
UNSALTED BUTTER

⅓ CUP MAPLE SYRUP

⅛ TEASPOON KOSHER SALT

2 CUPS WALNUT HALVES

1   Preheat the oven to 375°F and line a baking sheet with parchment paper.

2   Place the butter in a skillet and melt over medium heat. Stir in the maple syrup and salt and simmer until the mixture is frothy, about 3 minutes.

3   Add the walnuts and stir to coat. Cook, while stirring, for about 3 minutes.

4   Transfer the walnuts to the baking sheet, place them in the oven, and bake until caramelized, about 10 minutes. Remove, stir, and let cool until the coating hardens, about 30 minutes.

YIELD: 2 PINTS

ACTIVE TIME: 15 MINUTES

TOTAL TIME: 1 HOUR

PICKLED OKRA

1 LB. OKRA, TRIMMED

4 DRIED RED CHILI PEPPERS

2 BAY LEAVES

2 GARLIC CLOVES, HALVED

1 TEASPOON DILL SEEDS

1 TEASPOON
CORIANDER SEEDS

1 TEASPOON BLACK
PEPPERCORNS

1½ CUPS WATER

1½ CUPS APPLE
CIDER VINEGAR

1½ TABLESPOONS
KOSHER SALT

1   Divide the okra, chilies, bay leaves, garlic cloves, dill seeds, coriander seeds, and peppercorns evenly between two sterilized mason jars.

2   Place the water, vinegar, and salt in a saucepan and bring to a boil, stirring to dissolve the salt.

3   When the salt has dissolved, pour the brine into the jars, leaving ½ inch of space free at the top. To can the pickled okra, see page 38. If you do not want to can the okra, let cool completely before storing in the refrigerator, where they will keep for up to 2 weeks.

YIELD: 2 LOAVES

ACTIVE TIME: 10 MINUTES

TOTAL TIME: 1 HOUR AND 10 MINUTES

STOUT BREAD

⅓ CUP UNSALTED BUTTER, MELTED, PLUS MORE AS NEEDED

2¼ CUPS WHOLE WHEAT FLOUR

1 CUP ROLLED OATS, PLUS MORE AS NEEDED

½ CUP GENTLY PACKED BROWN SUGAR

2¼ TEASPOONS BAKING SODA

1 TEASPOON BAKING POWDER

½ TEASPOON KOSHER SALT

1 CUP BUTTERMILK

1 (12 OZ.) BOTTLE OF GUINNESS STOUT

1   Preheat the oven to 400°F and grease two 9 x 5–inch loaf pans with butter. Combine the dry ingredients in a bowl and set aside. In a separate bowl, combine the butter, buttermilk, and beer. Gradually add the dry mixture to the wet mixture and stir until thoroughly combined.

2   Divide the dough between the loaf pans and sprinkle additional oats on top. Place the pans in the oven and bake for 1 hour, until a knife inserted into the centers of the loaves comes out clean. Remove and let the pans cool on a wire rack before slicing and serving.

RUNZAS

FOR THE DOUGH

¾ CUP LUKEWARM
WATER (90°F)

1 TEASPOON ACTIVE
DRY YEAST

½ CUP SWEETENED
CONDENSED MILK

¼ CUP OLIVE OIL

2 TABLESPOONS SUGAR

1 LARGE EGG

3½ CUPS ALL-PURPOSE FLOUR,
PLUS MORE FOR DUSTING

1 TEASPOON KOSHER SALT

FOR THE FILLING

6 TABLESPOONS
UNSALTED BUTTER

1½ LBS. GROUND BEEF

1 YELLOW ONION, MINCED

2½ CUPS CHOPPED
GREEN CABBAGE

SALT AND PEPPER, TO TASTE

1 To prepare the dough, place the water and yeast in the mixing bowl of a stand mixer and let it stand until it is foamy, about 5 minutes. Fit a stand mixer with the dough hook attachment, add the remaining ingredients, and mix on low speed until the dough just holds together. Increase the speed to medium and mix until the dough is a ball and no longer sticks to the mixing bowl. Cover with a damp cloth and let rest until it doubles in size, about 1 hour.

2 To prepare the filling, place 1 tablespoon of the butter in a large skillet and melt over medium-high heat. Add the ground beef and cook, while using a fork to break it up, until it is browned, about 6 minutes. Place the beef on a paper towel–lined plate to drain, wipe out the skillet, and add another tablespoon of butter. Melt over medium heat, add the onion, and cook until it has softened, about 5 minutes. Add the cabbage and cook until it starts to wilt. Return the meat to the pan, stir to combine, and season with salt and pepper. Let the mixture cool.

3 Place the dough on a flour-dusted work surface, cut it into eight pieces, and roll each one into a 6-inch circle. Place about ¾ cup of the cooled filling in the center of a circle, fold the dough over it, and crimp to seal. Place the handpies on a parchment-lined baking sheet, cover with plastic wrap, and let them rise for 30 minutes.

4 Preheat the oven to 350°F. Place the handpies in the oven and cook for 10 minutes. Melt the remaining butter in a skillet and set it aside. After 10 minutes, remove the baking sheet from the oven and brush the top of each handpie with some of the melted butter. Return to the oven and bake until golden brown, about 10 minutes. Remove and brush with any remaining butter before serving.

YIELD: 8 SERVINGS

ACTIVE TIME: 10 MINUTES

TOTAL TIME: 1 HOUR AND 30 MINUTES

PUMPKIN QUICHE

5 LARGE EGGS

1 CUP UNSWEETENED PUMPKIN PUREE

1 CUP CRÈME FRAÎCHE

½ CUP MILK

½ CUP HEAVY CREAM

1 CUP GRATED PARMESAN CHEESE, PLUS MORE FOR GARNISH

½ TEASPOON KOSHER SALT

½ TEASPOON BLACK PEPPER

1 PIECRUST, BLIND BAKED (SEE PAGE 37)

⅓ CUP FRESH SAGE LEAVES, FINELY CHOPPED

1 Preheat the oven to 350°F. Place the eggs, pumpkin puree, crème fraîche, milk, cream, Parmesan, salt, and pepper in a mixing bowl and stir to combine. Pour the mixture into the piecrust and gently shake the pie plate to distribute evenly. Sprinkle the sage leaves over the top.

2 Place the quiche in the oven and bake until it is puffy and golden brown, about 35 minutes. Remove and let cool for 10 minutes. Garnish with additional Parmesan before serving.

YIELD: 4 SERVINGS

ACTIVE TIME: 15 MINUTES

TOTAL TIME: 1 HOUR AND 30 MINUTES

SPICY CARROTS

1 LB. LARGE CARROTS, PEELED

1 CUP UNSEASONED
RICE VINEGAR

1 TEASPOON KOSHER SALT

2 TABLESPOONS SUGAR,
PLUS 2 TEASPOONS

1 CUP WATER

1 Wash the carrots and cut into matchsticks or rounds that are about the size of a quarter. Pat dry.

2 Place the vinegar, salt, sugar, and water in a bowl and stir until the sugar dissolves. Add the carrots to the mixture and marinate for at least 1 hour before serving.

3 Place the carrots and brine in a mason jar and store in the refrigerator for up to 5 days.

YIELD: 2 PINTS

ACTIVE TIME: 15 MINUTES

TOTAL TIME: 12 HOURS TO 2 DAYS

QUICK PICKLES

1 LB. CUCUMBERS, CARROTS, OR TOMATOES

2 SPRIGS OF FRESH HERBS

1 TO 2 TEASPOONS BLACK PEPPERCORNS, CORIANDER SEEDS, OR MUSTARD SEEDS

1 TEASPOON DRIED HERBS OR GROUND SPICES

2 GARLIC CLOVES, SLICED

1 CUP PREFERRED VINEGAR

1 CUP WATER

1 TABLESPOON KOSHER SALT

1 TABLESPOON GRANULATED SUGAR

1 Cut the vegetables into the desired shapes and sizes.

2 Divide the chosen herbs and spices, and the garlic between two sterilized mason jars.

3 Pack the vegetables into the jars, making sure there is ½ inch of space remaining at the top. Pack them in as tightly as you can without damaging the vegetables.

4 Combine the vinegar, water, salt, and sugar in a small saucepan and bring to a boil, while stirring to dissolve the salt and sugar. When they are dissolved, pour the brine over the vegetables, filling each jar to within ½ inch of the top. To can these pickles, see page 38. If you are not interested in canning, let cool completely before storing in the refrigerator, where they will keep for up to 2 weeks.

YIELD: 4 TO 6 SERVINGS

ACTIVE TIME: 5 MINUTES

TOTAL TIME: 10 MINUTES

CAST-IRON SHISHITO PEPPERS

OLIVE OIL, FOR FRYING

2 LBS. SHISHITO PEPPERS

SALT, TO TASTE

1   Add olive oil to a 12-inch cast-iron skillet until it is ¼ inch deep and warm over medium heat.

2   When the oil is shimmering, add the peppers and cook, while turning once or twice, until they are blistered and golden brown, about 8 minutes. Take care not to crowd the pan with the peppers, and work in batches if necessary.

3   Transfer the blistered peppers to a paper towel–lined plate and season with salt.

NOTE: Eating shishito peppers is a bit like putting your taste buds through a round of Russian roulette, since approximately one in every 10 is spicy, and there's no way to tell until you bite down. The rest are as mild as can be.

YIELD: 1 CUP
ACTIVE TIME: 5 MINUTES
TOTAL TIME: 15 MINUTES

SALSA VERDE

6 TOMATILLOS, HUSKED AND RINSED

8 SERRANO PEPPERS, STEMMED AND SEEDED TO TASTE

½ YELLOW ONION, CHOPPED

2 GARLIC CLOVES, MINCED

SALT, TO TASTE

¼ CUP OLIVE OIL

FRESH CILANTRO, FINELY CHOPPED, FOR GARNISH

1   Place the tomatillos and serrano peppers in a large saucepan and cover with water. Bring to a boil and cook until the tomatillos start to lose their bright green color, about 10 minutes.

2   Drain and transfer the tomatillos and peppers to a blender. Add all of the remaining ingredients, except for the cilantro, and puree until smooth. Top with the cilantro and serve. The salsa will keep in the refrigerator for up to 2 days.

YIELD: 8 SERVINGS

ACTIVE TIME: 5 MINUTES

TOTAL TIME: 1 HOUR

BEER CHEESE DIP

1 LB. CHEDDAR
CHEESE, GRATED

4 OZ. CREAM CHEESE, AT
ROOM TEMPERATURE

1 GARLIC CLOVE, GRATED

¼ CUP RED WINE

1 TABLESPOON WHOLE
GRAIN MUSTARD

1 TEASPOON DIJON MUSTARD

2 TEASPOONS
WORCESTERSHIRE SAUCE

½ TEASPOON PAPRIKA

1 CUP BROWN ALE

1   Place all of the ingredients, except for the beer, in a food processor and blitz until well combined.

2   Pour in ½ cup of the beer and blitz until incorporated. Gradually add the rest of the beer, blitzing to incorporate each portion before adding another.

3   Transfer to a bowl, cover with plastic wrap, and refrigerate for 1 hour before serving.

YIELD: 2 CUPS
ACTIVE TIME: 5 MINUTES
TOTAL TIME: 15 MINUTES

DRIED-FRUIT CHUTNEY

1 SHALLOT, MINCED

1 TABLESPOON
CORIANDER SEEDS

1-INCH PIECE OF FRESH
GINGER, PEELED AND MINCED

1 TEASPOON OLIVE OIL

1½ CUPS CHOPPED
DRIED APRICOTS

1 CUP APPLE CIDER VINEGAR

¼ CUP CHOPPED DRIED FIGS

¼ CUP CHOPPED PRUNES

¼ CUP GOLDEN RAISINS

¼ CUP DARK MOLASSES

1½ CUPS WATER

SALT AND PEPPER, TO TASTE

1　Place the shallot, coriander, ginger, and oil in a medium saucepan and cook over medium heat until the mixture is fragrant, about 1 minute.

2　Add the apricots, vinegar, figs, prunes, raisins, molasses, and water to the saucepan, season with salt and pepper, and simmer the mixture until the fruit is soft and the liquid has almost evaporated. Remove from heat and let cool before serving. The chutney will keep in the refrigerator for up to 1 week.

YIELD: 1 CUPS
ACTIVE TIME: 15 MINUTES
TOTAL TIME: 15 MINUTES

HUMMUS

1 (14 OZ.) CAN OF CHICKPEAS

3 TABLESPOONS EXTRA
VIRGIN OLIVE OIL

3 TABLESPOONS TAHINI

1½ TABLESPOONS FRESH
LEMON JUICE, PLUS MORE
TO TASTE

1 GARLIC CLOVE, CHOPPED

1 TEASPOON KOSHER SALT

½ TEASPOON BLACK PEPPER

1 Drain the chickpeas and reserve the liquid. If time allows, remove the skins from each of the chickpeas. This will make your hummus much smoother.

2 Place the chickpeas, olive oil, tahini, lemon juice, garlic, salt, and pepper in a food processor and blitz until the mixture is very smooth, scraping down the work bowl as needed.

3 Taste and adjust the seasoning. If your hummus is stiffer than you'd like, add 2 to 3 tablespoons of the reserved chickpea liquid and blitz until it is the desired consistency.

HUMMUS VARIATIONS

For a more authentic hummus, soak dried chickpeas and 1 tablespoon baking soda overnight and then cook them for 1 hour, with an additional tablespoon of baking soda. You can also dress it up with any of the following options: add 1 to 3 teaspoons of spices like cumin, sumac, harissa, or smoked paprika; drizzle a little pomegranate molasses on top; blend in 1 cup of roasted eggplant, zucchini, bell peppers, or garlic; or fold in ¾ cup of chopped green or black olives.

YIELD: 8 SERVINGS

ACTIVE TIME: 5 MINUTES

TOTAL TIME: 35 MINUTES

PUMPKIN SPREAD

1 (3 LB.) SUGAR PUMPKIN, HALVED AND SEEDED

1 TABLESPOON OLIVE OIL

2 TEASPOONS KOSHER SALT

1 TEASPOON BLACK PEPPER

¼ CUP OLIVE OIL

1 TEASPOON FINELY CHOPPED FRESH THYME

¼ TEASPOON GRATED FRESH NUTMEG

¼ CUP GRATED PARMESAN CHEESE

1 TABLESPOON FRESH LEMON JUICE

1 TABLESPOON PLAIN GREEK YOGURT

1 Preheat the oven to 425°F. Place the pumpkin, cut-side up, on a parchment-lined baking sheet and brush it with the olive oil. Sprinkle half of the salt over the pumpkin, place it in the oven, and roast for 25 to 30 minutes, until the flesh is tender. Remove from the oven and let the pumpkin cool.

2 When the pumpkin is cool enough to handle, scrape the flesh into a food processor. Add the remaining ingredients and puree until smooth.

YIELD: ½ CUP

ACTIVE TIME: 30 MINUTES

TOTAL TIME: 2 HOURS AND 45 MINUTES

CARAMELIZED ONION MAYONNAISE

2 TABLESPOONS
UNSALTED BUTTER

2 SWEET ONIONS,
SLICED THIN

SALT AND PEPPER, TO TASTE

½ CUP MAYONNAISE

1 Place the butter in a skillet and melt over medium-low heat.

2 Add the onions and a pinch of salt and cook, while stirring frequently, until the onions develop a deep brown color, about 35 minutes. Remove from heat and let cool completely.

3 Transfer the cooled onions to a blender and puree until smooth. Place the puree and mayonnaise in a mixing bowl, season with salt and pepper, and stir to combine. Place the mixture in the refrigerator for at least 2 hours before serving.

CULTURED BUTTER

4 CUPS HIGH-QUALITY
HEAVY CREAM

½ CUP WHOLE MILK YOGURT

½ TEASPOON KOSHER SALT

1 Place the heavy cream and yogurt in a jar. Seal the jar and shake vigorously.

2 Open the jar, cover with cheesecloth, and secure with a rubber band or kitchen twine.

3 Place the mixture away from direct sunlight and let it sit at room temperature for 36 hours.

4 After 36 hours, seal the jar and place it in the refrigerator for 4 to 6 hours.

5 Remove the mixture from the refrigerator and pour into the work bowl of a stand mixer fitted with the whisk attachment. Whip on high, covering with a towel to prevent spilling, until the butter separates from the buttermilk. Reserve the buttermilk for another preparation.

6 Transfer the butter to a cheesecloth and squeeze out any excess liquid. Wash the butter under ice-cold water and store in an airtight container. It will keep in the refrigerator for approximately 3 months.

YIELD: 4 SERVINGS

ACTIVE TIME: 20 MINUTES

TOTAL TIME: 1 HOUR AND 30 MINUTES

EGGPLANT DIP

1 LARGE ITALIAN EGGPLANT, HALVED LENGTHWISE

1 TABLESPOON OLIVE OIL, PLUS MORE AS NEEDED

1 ONION, DICED

2 GARLIC CLOVES, CHOPPED

1 TABLESPOON REAL MAPLE SYRUP

FRESH LEMON JUICE, TO TASTE

SALT AND PEPPER, TO TASTE

2 TABLESPOONS CHOPPED TOMATO

1 TABLESPOON FINELY CHOPPED FRESH PARSLEY OR CILANTRO

1 TABLESPOON DUKKAH

1 Preheat oven to 350°F. Place the eggplant, cut-side down, on a greased baking sheet. Place in the oven and roast until the skin is blistered and the flesh is very tender, about 30 minutes. Remove from the oven and let cool.

2 Place the oil in a skillet and warm over medium heat. When the oil starts to shimmer, add the onion and cook until it starts to brown, about 7 minutes. Add the garlic and cook for 2 minutes.

3 Remove the skin from the cooled eggplant and add the flesh to the pan. Cook the eggplant until it breaks down further and becomes extremely tender, about 5 minutes.

4 Remove from the heat and add the maple syrup, lemon juice, salt, and pepper. For a smoother dip, puree the mixture. Otherwise, leave chunky. Let the mixture cool.

5 When cool, place it in a small bowl and top with the tomatoes, parsley or cilantro, and dukkah.

YIELD: 1 CUP
ACTIVE TIME: 5 MINUTES
TOTAL TIME: 5 MINUTES

ROMESCO SAUCE

2 LARGE ROASTED RED
BELL PEPPERS

1 GARLIC CLOVE, SMASHED

½ CUP SLIVERED
ALMONDS, TOASTED

¼ CUP TOMATO PUREE

2 TABLESPOONS FINELY
CHOPPED FRESH PARSLEY

2 TABLESPOONS
SHERRY VINEGAR

1 TEASPOON
SMOKED PAPRIKA

SALT AND PEPPER, TO TASTE

½ CUP OLIVE OIL

1   Place all of the ingredients, except for the olive oil, in a blender or food processor and pulse until the mixture is smooth.

2   Add the olive oil in a steady stream and blitz until emulsified. Season with salt and pepper and serve.

YIELD: 2 CUPS

ACTIVE TIME: 5 MINUTES

TOTAL TIME: 35 MINUTES

WHITE BEAN SPREAD

1 (14 OZ.) CAN OF CANNELLINI
BEANS, DRAINED AND RINSED

2 TABLESPOONS OLIVE OIL

2 TEASPOONS
BALSAMIC VINEGAR

2 GARLIC CLOVES, MINCED

1 TABLESPOON FINELY
CHOPPED FRESH ROSEMARY

½ CELERY STALK, MINCED

SALT AND PEPPER, TO TASTE

2 PINCHES OF RED
PEPPER FLAKES

1   Place half of the beans in a mixing bowl and mash them. Add the rest of the beans, the olive oil, vinegar, garlic, rosemary, and celery and stir to combine.

2   Season with salt, pepper, and red pepper flakes and cover the bowl with plastic wrap. Let stand for about 30 minutes before serving.

YIELD: 1½ CUPS

ACTIVE TIME: 5 MINUTES

TOTAL TIME: 1 HOUR

CRANBERRY JAM

½ LB. FRESH CRANBERRIES

½ CUP SUGAR

½ CUP APPLE CIDER

½-INCH PIECE OF FRESH
GINGER, PEELED AND MINCED

1 TEASPOON ORANGE ZEST

½ TEASPOON KOSHER SALT

1 Place all of the ingredients in a small saucepan and bring to a boil. Reduce the heat so that the mixture simmers and cook until the mixture has reduced, 20 to 25 minutes.

2 Transfer the mixture to a sterilized mason jar. To can this jam, see page 38. If you do not want to can the jam, let it cool completely before storing in the refrigerator, where it will keep for up to 1 week.

YIELD: 6 SERVINGS

ACTIVE TIME: 15 MINUTES

TOTAL TIME: 1 HOUR

BAKED APPLES

6 APPLES

3 TABLESPOONS UNSALTED
BUTTER, MELTED

6 TABLESPOONS
BLACKBERRY JAM

2 OZ. GOAT CHEESE

1   Preheat the oven to 350°F. Slice the tops off of the apples and set aside. Use a paring knife to cut a circle around the apples' cores and then scoop out their centers. Make sure to leave a ½-inch-thick wall inside the apple.

2   Rub the inside and outside of the apples with some of the melted butter. Place the jam and goat cheese in a mixing bowl and stir to combine. Fill the apples' cavities with the mixture, place the tops back on the apples, and set them aside.

3   Warm a cast-iron skillet over medium-high heat. Add the remaining butter, place the apples in the skillet, and place the skillet in the oven. Bake the apples until tender, 25 to 30 minutes. Remove from the oven and let cool briefly before serving.

YIELD: 24 TWISTS
ACTIVE TIME: 15 MINUTES
TOTAL TIME: 30 MINUTES

CINNAMON TWISTS

2 SHEETS OF FROZEN PUFF
PASTRY, THAWED

ALL-PURPOSE FLOUR,
AS NEEDED

1 CUP SUGAR

3½ TABLESPOONS CINNAMON

1 TEASPOON GRATED
FRESH NUTMEG

1 EGG

1 Preheat oven to 375°F and line a baking sheet with parchment paper. Place the sheets of puff pastry on a flour-dusted work surface and roll them out into 12 x 10–inch rectangles.

2 Place the sugar, cinnamon, and nutmeg in a bowl. Beat the egg in a separate bowl.

3 Lightly brush the top of each pastry sheet with the egg and then sprinkle the sugar-and-spice mixture over the pastry.

4 Cut the pastries into long strips and twist them. Place the twists on a parchment-lined baking sheet and bake for about 12 minutes, until golden brown. Remove from the oven, flip the twists over, and bake for an additional 2 to 3 minutes. Remove from the oven and let cool slightly before serving.

WHOOPIE PIES

2½ STICKS OF UNSALTED BUTTER, AT ROOM TEMPERATURE

1¼ CUPS CONFECTIONERS' SUGAR

2 PINCHES OF KOSHER SALT

2½ TEASPOONS PURE VANILLA EXTRACT

2½ CUPS MARSHMALLOW CRÈME

2 CUPS ALL-PURPOSE FLOUR

½ CUP UNSWEETENED COCOA POWDER

1 TEASPOON BAKING SODA

1 CUP GENTLY PACKED LIGHT BROWN SUGAR

1 LARGE EGG, AT ROOM TEMPERATURE

1 CUP BUTTERMILK

1 Place 12 tablespoons of the butter and the confectioners' sugar in a mixing bowl and beat until the mixture is fluffy. Add a pinch of salt and 1½ teaspoons of the vanilla and beat until combined. Add the marshmallow crème and beat until incorporated. Place the filling in the refrigerator and chill for at least 30 minutes.

2 Preheat the oven to 350°F.

3 Place the flour, cocoa powder, baking soda, and the remaining salt in a bowl and whisk to combine. Place the remaining butter and the brown sugar in another mixing bowl and beat until the mixture is fluffy. Add the egg, beat until incorporated, and then add the remaining vanilla.

4 Gradually add the dry mixture and the buttermilk, alternating between them. Beat until incorporated and then scoop the batter onto parchment-lined baking sheets, making sure to leave plenty of room between the scoops.

5 Place the sheets in the oven and bake, while rotating and switching their positions halfway through, for 15 minutes. The cakes should feel springy to the touch when done. Remove from the oven and let cool on the baking sheets.

6 Place the filling in the center of one cake, top with another cake, and press down to spread the filling to the edges. Repeat with the remaining filling and cakes and then serve.

YIELD: 16 TRUFFLES

ACTIVE TIME: 10 MINUTES

TOTAL TIME: 2 HOURS

HONEY NUT TRUFFLES

½ CUP PEANUT BUTTER

¼ CUP HONEY

¼ TEASPOON KOSHER SALT

1 CUP HIGH-QUALITY SEMISWEET CHOCOLATE CHIPS

1 Place the peanut butter, honey, and salt in a bowl and stir until well combined. Form teaspoons of the mixture into balls, place them on a parchment-lined baking sheet, and refrigerate for 1 hour.

2 Remove the baking sheet from the refrigerator. Place the chocolate chips in a microwave-safe bowl and microwave until melted, removing to stir every 15 seconds.

3 Dip the balls into the melted chocolate until completely coated. Place them back on the baking sheet. When all of the truffles have been coated, place them in the refrigerator and chill until the chocolate is set.

YIELD: 24 COOKIES

ACTIVE TIME: 30 MINUTES

TOTAL TIME: 1 HOUR AND 45 MINUTES

MACARONS

3 EGG WHITES

¼ CUP GRANULATED SUGAR

1⅔ CUPS CONFECTIONERS' SUGAR

1 CUP FINELY GROUND ALMONDS

2 TO 3 DROPS OF PREFERRED GEL FOOD COLORING

1 Line a baking sheet with parchment paper.

2 Place the egg whites in the work bowl of a stand mixer fitted with the whisk attachment. Beat until foamy, add the granulated sugar, and continue to beat until the mixture is glossy, fluffy, and holds soft peaks.

3 Sift the confectioners' sugar and the ground almonds into a separate bowl. Add this mixture and the gel food coloring into the egg white mixture and fold until incorporated, taking care not to overmix the batter.

4 Transfer the batter into a resealable plastic bag with one corner removed. Pipe a 1½-inch disk of batter onto the parchment-lined baking sheet. If the disk holds a peak instead of flattening immediately, gently fold the batter a few more times and retest. Repeat until the disk flattens into an even disk. Transfer the batter into a piping bag fitted with a standard tip.

5 Pipe the batter onto the parchment-lined baking sheet. Let stand at room temperature until a skin forms on the tops of the disks, about 1 hour.

6 Preheat the oven to 275°F. Place the cookies in the oven and bake until they are set but not browned, about 10 minutes. Remove and let cool completely before filling.

IT'S WHAT'S INSIDE THAT COUNTS

The macaron can accommodate a large number of fillings, and thus appeal to a wide spectrum of palates. While you shouldn't be afraid to be bold with your filling decisions, always remember to err on the dry side, as wetter fillings, such as whipped cream, will dissolve the cookie. To get your mind working, here are a few standard fillings.

CHOCOLATE GANACHE: Heat ½ cup heavy cream in a saucepan and bring to a simmer. Stir in ¼ pound of chopped dark chocolate and continue stirring until the chocolate is melted. Add 2 tablespoons of unsalted butter, stir until the mixture is smooth, and chill in the refrigerator until thick and cool.

VANILLA BUTTERCREAM: Place 10 tablespoons unsalted butter in a mixing bowl and beat at medium speed with a handheld mixer fitted with a whisk attachment until smooth. Add 1½ teaspoons pure vanilla extract, 1¼ cups confectioners' sugar, and a pinch of kosher salt and beat until the mixture is fully combined. Scrape down the bowl as needed while mixing. Add 1 tablespoon heavy cream and beat until the mixture is light and fluffy, about 4 minutes, stopping to scrape down the bowl as needed.

RASPBERRY BUTTERCREAM: Add ¼ cup of seedless raspberry jam to the Vanilla Buttercream and beat until incorporated.

LEMON CURD: Place 1 cup fresh lemon juice, 4 teaspoons of lemon zest, 6 large eggs, 1⅓ cups sugar, and 2 sticks of unsalted butter in the work bowl of a stand mixer fitted with the paddle attachment. Beat on medium speed until well combined. Pour the mixture into a saucepan and cook over low heat until it is thick enough to coat the back of a wooden spoon, about 10 minutes. Pour the lemon curd into a bowl, place it in the refrigerator, and chill until it thickens to a custard-like consistency.

YIELD: 8 SERVINGS

ACTIVE TIME: 15 MINUTES

TOTAL TIME: 30 MINUTES

RUSTICO WITH HONEY GLAZE

VEGETABLE OIL, FOR FRYING

4 SHEETS OF FROZEN PUFF
PASTRY, THAWED

1 EGG WHITE, BEATEN

½ LB. FRESH MOZZARELLA
CHEESE, SLICED

1 CUP HONEY

1 Add vegetable oil to a Dutch oven until it is 2 inches deep and bring to 350°F over medium-high heat.

2 Cut eight 5-inch circles and eight 4-inch circles from the sheets of puff pastry. Brush the circles with the egg white.

3 Place a slice of cheese in the center of each 5-inch circle. Place a 4-inch circle over the cheese, fold the large circle over the edge, and pinch to seal.

4 Place one or two rustico in the oil and fry until the dough is a light golden brown and crispy, about 2 to 3 minutes. Remove from oil and transfer to a paper towel–lined wire rack. Repeat until all the pastries have been fried. Drizzle the honey over the top and serve.

WINTER

As anyone from a northern clime knows, the need for warmth, comfort, and fun is at its peak in the winter. When the need for all those things arises, the best antidote is food, friends, and family, and, it just so happens, they all tend to gravitate around a lovingly arranged serving board.

A serving board or platter, and the conversations that inevitably arise around them, will wash away the blues everyone's built up, and set their sights on the good things the world contains. Focusing on filling recipes and those sweet treats that everyone seems to crave once the holiday season rolls around, we make sure what's happening outside has no control over what's happening inside.

HERB CRACKERS

2 CUPS ALL-PURPOSE FLOUR,
PLUS MORE AS NEEDED

1½ TEASPOONS
BAKING POWDER

1 CUP WATER

3 TABLESPOONS OLIVE OIL,
PLUS MORE AS NEEDED

1 TEASPOON SEA SALT, PLUS
MORE TO TASTE

1 TEASPOON PAPRIKA

1 TEASPOON BLACK PEPPER

FRESH HERBS,
FINELY CHOPPED

1   Place all of the ingredients, except for the herbs, in a mixing bowl and stir until thoroughly combined. Cover the bowl and refrigerate the mixture for 1 hour.

2   Preheat the oven to 425°F and line a baking sheet with parchment paper.

3   Form the dough into small balls. Place them on a flour-dusted work surface and roll them out into long, paper-thin rectangles.

4   Place the crackers on a baking sheet and brush their surfaces with a generous amount of olive oil. Sprinkle the salt and fresh herbs over the top. Place in the oven and bake for 5 minutes, until the crackers are crispy and golden brown. Remove and let the crackers cool on a wire rack before serving.

FETA-FILLED PEPPADEW PEPPERS

1 (14 OZ.) JAR OF PEPPADEW PEPPERS

½ LB. FETA CHEESE

¼ CUP OLIVE OIL

¼ CUP FINELY CHOPPED FRESH BASIL

1   Drain the peppadew peppers, but don't rinse them. Carefully stuff the feta cheese into the peppers' cavities, taking care not to tear the delicate peppers, and place them on a plate.

2   Drizzle olive oil over the stuffed peppers and sprinkle the basil on top.

YIELD: 6 EGGS

ACTIVE TIME: 15 MINUTES

TOTAL TIME: 30 MINUTES

DEVILED EGGS WITH SPAM

6 HARD-BOILED EGGS

2 TABLESPOONS YELLOW MUSTARD

2 TABLESPOONS MAYONNAISE

2 TEASPOONS WHOLE GRAIN MUSTARD

2 CORNICHONS, DICED

2 TEASPOONS PIMENTOS

SALT AND PEPPER, TO TASTE

FRESH PARSLEY, FINELY CHOPPED, FOR GARNISH

FRESH DILL, FINELY CHOPPED, FOR GARNISH

1 SLICE OF SPAM, FRIED AND CUT INTO TRIANGLES, FOR GARNISH (OPTIONAL)

1 Cut the eggs in half, remove the yolks, and place them in a small bowl. Add all of the ingredients, except for the garnishes, and stir until thoroughly combined.

2 Spoon the yolk mixture into the cavities in the egg whites. Garnish with parsley, dill, and, if desired, the Spam.

YIELD: 10 TO 15 SERVINGS
ACTIVE TIME: 20 MINUTES
TOTAL TIME: 24 HOURS

PORK PÂTÉ

3- TO 5-LB. BONE-IN
PORK SHOULDER

3 ONIONS, SLICED

2 TEASPOONS
GROUND CLOVES

1 TABLESPOON KOSHER SALT,
PLUS MORE TO TASTE

4 BAY LEAVES

2 TEASPOONS BLACK PEPPER,
PLUS MORE TO TASTE

1 TEASPOON GRATED
FRESH NUTMEG

1 Preheat the oven to 300°F. Place all of the ingredients in a Dutch oven and stir to combine. Cover, place in the oven, and braise until the pork falls apart at the touch of a fork, about 3 to 4 hours.

2 Remove from the oven, discard the bay leaves, and transfer the pork shoulder to a plate. When the pork shoulder has cooled slightly, shred it with a fork.

3 Place the shredded pork and ½ cup of the cooking liquid in a blender. Puree until it forms a paste, adding more cooking liquid as needed to achieve the desired consistency.

4 Season with salt and pepper, transfer the paste to a large jar, and then pour the remaining cooking liquid over it. Cover the jar and store it in the refrigerator overnight before serving.

YIELD: 4 TO 6 SERVINGS

ACTIVE TIME: 5 MINUTES

TOTAL TIME: 15 MINUTES

CARAWAY WATER BISCUITS

2 TABLESPOONS
ALL-PURPOSE FLOUR

10 TABLESPOONS WATER

⅛ TEASPOON KOSHER SALT

2 TABLESPOONS
CARAWAY SEEDS

1 Preheat the oven to 350°F and line a baking sheet with parchment paper.

2 Place the flour and water in a mixing bowl and whisk until combined. Stir in the salt.

3 Use a pastry brush to transfer the batter to the baking sheet, taking care to make nice, long crackers.

4 Sprinkle caraway seeds over the crackers and place them in the oven. Bake for 8 minutes, or until golden brown. Remove the sheet and let the crackers cool before serving.

YIELD: 6 SERVINGS

ACTIVE TIME: 5 MINUTES

TOTAL TIME: 20 MINUTES

PURPLE POTATO CHIPS

3 LARGE PURPLE POTATOES, SLICED THIN

¼ CUP OLIVE OIL

2 TEASPOONS SEA SALT

1 Preheat the oven to 400°F.

2 Place the potatoes and the olive oil in a bowl and toss until the potatoes are evenly coated. Place the potatoes on a baking sheet in a single layer. Bake for 12 to 15 minutes, until crispy.

3 Remove from the oven, transfer to a bowl, sprinkle the salt over the chips, and gently toss. Serve warm or store in an airtight container for up to 1 week.

YIELD: 4 SERVINGS

ACTIVE TIME: 5 MINUTES

TOTAL TIME: 20 MINUTES

BEET CHIPS

5 BEETS, PEELED AND
SLICED VERY THIN

¼ CUP OLIVE OIL

2 TEASPOONS SEA SALT

1 Preheat the oven to 400°F.

2 Place the beets and olive oil in a bowl and toss until the slices are evenly coated. Place them on parchment-lined baking sheets in a single layer. Bake for 12 to 15 minutes, or until crispy.

3 Remove from the oven, transfer to a bowl, add the salt, and gently toss to coat. Serve warm or store in an airtight container for up to 1 week.

YIELD: 6 SERVINGS

ACTIVE TIME: 15 MINUTES

TOTAL TIME: 1 HOUR

BROWN BREAD

BUTTER, FOR GREASING

½ CUP RYE FLOUR

½ CUP ALL-PURPOSE FLOUR

½ CUP FINELY
GROUND CORNMEAL

½ TEASPOON ALLSPICE

½ TEASPOON
BAKING POWDER

½ TEASPOON BAKING SODA

½ CUP BLACKSTRAP
MOLASSES

¾ CUP BUTTERMILK

1   Preheat the oven to 325°F and grease a loaf pan with butter.

2   Sift the dry ingredients into a mixing bowl. Place the molasses and buttermilk in a separate mixing bowl and stir to combine. Add the wet mixture to the dry mixture and stir until well combined.

3   Pour the batter into the loaf pan and cover with foil.

4   Preheat the oven to 325°F. Place the loaf pan in the oven and bake for 40 to 45 minutes, until a knife inserted in the center comes out clean. Remove the bread from the oven and let cool completely before serving.

NOTE: This is traditionally prepared in a coffee can. To do this, place the can in a Dutch oven, add boiling water so that three-quarters of the can is submerged, cover the Dutch oven, and place in the oven until a knife inserted in the center of the bread comes out clean, about 2 hours. If you are going to steam the bread in this manner—and with the light, moist bread that results, it's worth considering—make sure you check the water level after 1 hour, adding more if needed.

YIELD: 2 CUPS

ACTIVE TIME: 10 MINUTES

TOTAL TIME: 30 MINUTES

ROASTED ALMONDS

½ TEASPOON KOSHER SALT

2 CUPS ALMONDS

LEAVES FROM 3 SPRIGS
OF FRESH THYME

LEAVES FROM 1 SPRIG OF
FRESH SUMMER SAVORY

2 TEASPOONS OLIVE OIL

1   Preheat the oven to 375°F.

2   Place all of the ingredients in a mixing bowl and stir to combine.

3   Place the almonds in single layer on a baking sheet and roast for 15 to 20 minutes, removing to stir every 5 minutes. Once the almonds have browned, remove them from the oven and let cool before serving.

YIELD: 8 SERVINGS

ACTIVE TIME: 5 MINUTES

TOTAL TIME: 1 HOUR

ROASTED CHESTNUTS

1 LB. CHESTNUTS

½ TEASPOON KOSHER SALT

¼ TEASPOON BLACK PEPPER

2 TABLESPOONS UNSALTED BUTTER, MELTED

1 TABLESPOON OLIVE OIL

3 SPRIGS OF FRESH THYME

1 CINNAMON STICK

2 WHOLE CLOVES

1 Preheat the oven to 425°F. Carve an "X" on the rounded side of each chestnut and place them in a bowl of hot water. Soak for about 1 minute.

2 Drain the chestnuts and create an aluminum foil pouch. Place the chestnuts in the pouch, sprinkle salt and pepper over them, drizzle with the butter and olive oil on top, and add the thyme, cinnamon stick, and cloves to the pouch. Close the pouch, leaving an opening so that steam can escape.

3 Place in the oven and roast for 40 to 45 minutes, until the chestnuts are tender. Remove from the oven and serve warm.

YIELD: 4 SERVINGS

ACTIVE TIME: 15 MINUTES

TOTAL TIME: 20 MINUTES

ONION RINGS

½ CUP ALL-PURPOSE FLOUR

1 EGG, BEATEN

⅓ CUP WHOLE MILK

½ TEASPOON PAPRIKA

½ CUP BREAD CRUMBS

½ CUP PANKO

1 TABLESPOON GRATED
PARMESAN CHEESE

VEGETABLE OIL, FOR FRYING

2 LARGE YELLOW ONIONS,
SLICED INTO THICK RINGS

SALT, TO TASTE

1 Place the flour in a shallow bowl. Place the beaten egg, milk, and paprika in another, and the bread crumbs and Parmesan in another.

2 Place a Dutch oven on the stove and add vegetable oil until it is 2 inches deep. Heat the oil until a few bread crumbs sizzle immediately when dropped in.

3 Dip the onions in the flour, then in the egg mixture, and lastly in the bread crumb mixture until fully coated. Carefully drop them into the hot oil and fry, turning over once, until they are golden brown all over, 4 to 5 minutes.

4 Transfer the onion rings to a paper towel–lined plate, sprinkle salt over them, and let cool briefly before serving.

YIELD: 4 SERVINGS

ACTIVE TIME: 5 MINUTES

TOTAL TIME: 10 MINUTES

ROASTED SEAWEED SNACKS

SHEETS OF NORI SEAWEED,
AS NEEDED

TOASTED SESAME OIL,
AS NEEDED

SALT, TO TASTE

PREFERRED SEASONINGS,
TO TASTE

1   Preheat the oven to 400°F. Take a sheet of seaweed and brush both sides liberally with sesame oil. Sprinkle with salt and any other seasonings and place them on a baking sheet. Repeat with as many sheets as will fit on the sheet.

2   Put the baking sheet in the oven and roast for 5 minutes. Turn the sheets of seaweed over and roast for another 5 minutes. Remove and let cool briefly before serving.

YIELD: 4 TO 6 SERVINGS

ACTIVE TIME: 45 MINUTES

TOTAL TIME: 1 HOUR AND 15 MINUTES

TIROPITAKIA

½ LB. FETA CHEESE

1 CUP GRATED
KEFALOTYRI CHEESE

¼ CUP FINELY CHOPPED
FRESH PARSLEY

2 EGGS, BEATEN

BLACK PEPPER, TO TASTE

1 (1 LB.) PACKAGE OF FROZEN
PHYLLO DOUGH, THAWED

2 STICKS OF UNSALTED
BUTTER, MELTED

1   Place the feta cheese in a mixing bowl and break it up with a fork. Add the kefalotyri, parsley, eggs, and pepper and stir to combine. Set the mixture aside.

2   Place 1 sheet of the phyllo dough on a large sheet of parchment paper. Gently brush the sheet with some of the melted butter, place another sheet on top, and brush this with more of the butter. Cut the phyllo dough into 2-inch strips, place 1 teaspoon of the filling at the end of the strip closest to you, and fold over one corner to make a triangle. Fold the strip up until the filling is completely encased. Repeat with the remaining sheets of phyllo dough and filling.

3   Preheat the oven to 350°F and grease a baking sheet with some of the melted butter. Place the pastries on the baking sheet and bake in the oven until golden brown, about 15 minutes. Remove and let cool briefly before serving.

YIELD: 8 SERVINGS
ACTIVE TIME: 15 MINUTES
TOTAL TIME: 2 HOURS

BACON & ZUCCHINI QUICHE

8 SLICES OF THICK-CUT BACON, COOKED AND CHOPPED

1 PIECRUST, BLIND BAKED (SEE PAGE 37)

1 TABLESPOON OLIVE OIL

1 SMALL ZUCCHINI, TRIMMED AND SLICED INTO THIN ROUNDS

1 GARLIC CLOVE, MINCED

4 OZ. GARLIC & HERB GOAT CHEESE

4 EGGS

1 CUP HALF-AND-HALF

½ TEASPOON KOSHER SALT

½ TEASPOON BLACK PEPPER

1   Preheat the oven to 350°F. Sprinkle the bacon over the crust and set aside.

2   Place the olive oil in a skillet and warm over medium-high heat. When the oil starts to shimmer, add the zucchini and cook until it has softened, about 10 minutes. Add the garlic and cook for another minute. Spoon the mixture over the bacon in the piecrust. Dot the mixture with the goat cheese and set aside.

3   Place the eggs, half-and-half, salt, and pepper in a mixing bowl and whisk to combine. Pour the egg mixture into the piecrust and gently shake the pie plate to distribute evenly.

4   Place the quiche in the oven and bake for 35 minutes, until the quiche is puffy and golden brown. Remove from the oven and let cool for 10 minutes before serving.

BAKED BRIE, TWO WAYS

½ LB. WHEEL OF BRIE CHEESE

FOR THE SAVORY TOPPING

¼ CUP CHOPPED
ROASTED TOMATOES

¼ CUP CHOPPED
ARTICHOKE HEARTS

2 TABLESPOONS PITTED
AND CHOPPED OLIVES

1 TABLESPOON CAPERS

PINCH OF BLACK PEPPER

FOR THE SWEET TOPPING

¼ CUP CHOPPED PECANS

¼ CUP CHOPPED
DRIED APRICOTS

⅓ CUP DIVINA FIG SPREAD

¼ CUP DRIED CHERRIES

PINCH OF CINNAMON

1 Preheat the oven to 350°F.

2 Place the cheese in a ceramic dish and top it with your mixture of choice.

3 Place in the oven and bake for 15 minutes, until cheese is gooey.

4 Remove from the oven and serve.

YIELD: 6 SERVINGS

ACTIVE TIME: 10 MINUTES

TOTAL TIME: 20 MINUTES

FONDUE

1 LB. GRUYÈRE
CHEESE, GRATED

½ LB. EMMENTAL
CHEESE, GRATED

½ LB. GOUDA CHEESE, GRATED

2 TABLESPOONS
CORNSTARCH

1 GARLIC CLOVE, HALVED

1 CUP WHITE WINE

1 TABLESPOON FRESH
LEMON JUICE

SALT AND PEPPER, TO TASTE

GRATED FRESH NUTMEG,
TO TASTE

1 Place the cheeses and the cornstarch in a bowl and toss until the cheeses are evenly coated.

2 Rub the inside of the fondue pot with the garlic and place it over the flame to warm it up.

3 Place the wine and lemon juice in a saucepan and bring to a simmer over low heat. Add the cheese mixture and cook, stirring constantly, until the cheeses have melted and the mixture is smooth. Season with salt, pepper, and nutmeg, transfer the mixture to the fondue pot, and enjoy.

FONDUE FOLKLORE

A fun fondue tradition is to leave a thin layer of fondue at the bottom of the *caquelon* (fondue pot). By carefully controlling the heat, you can form this layer into a crust known as *La Religieuse*—"The Religious One." Lift it out and distribute it among your guests. You'll see why it is considered a delicacy.

YIELD: 4 CUPS

ACTIVE TIME: 10 MINUTES

TOTAL TIME: 10 MINUTES

BLACK BEAN SPREAD

2 (14 OZ.) CANS OF
BLACK BEANS

¼ CUP TAHINI

¾ CUP FRESH LIME JUICE

¾ CUP OLIVE OIL

2 TEASPOONS SEA SALT

1 TABLESPOON BLACK PEPPER

1 TEASPOON TABASCO

1 TEASPOON ANCHOVY PASTE

WATER, AS NEEDED

FRESH CILANTRO, FINELY
CHOPPED, FOR GARNISH

1　Place all of the ingredients, except for the cilantro, in a food processor and blend until the desired consistency is achieved. If too thick, add a tablespoon of water.

2　Place the hummus in a serving bowl, garnish with the cilantro, and serve.

YIELD: ½ CUP

ACTIVE TIME: 5 MINUTES

TOTAL TIME: 15 MINUTES

MOSTARDA

¼ LB. DRIED
APRICOTS, CHOPPED

¼ CUP CHOPPED
DRIED CHERRIES

1 SHALLOT, MINCED

1½ TEASPOONS MINCED
CRYSTALLIZED GINGER

½ CUP DRY WHITE WINE

3 TABLESPOONS WHITE
WINE VINEGAR

3 TABLESPOONS WATER

3 TABLESPOONS SUGAR

1 TEASPOON
MUSTARD POWDER

1 TEASPOON DIJON MUSTARD

1 TABLESPOON
UNSALTED BUTTER

1 Place the apricots, cherries, shallot, ginger, wine, vinegar, water, and sugar in a saucepan and bring to a boil over medium-high heat. Cover, reduce the heat to medium, and cook until all of the liquid has been absorbed and the fruit is soft, about 10 minutes.

2 Uncover the pot and stir in the mustard powder, Dijon mustard, and butter. Simmer until the mixture is jam-like, about 2 to 3 minutes. Remove from heat and let cool slightly before serving. The mostarda will keep in the refrigerator for up to 1 week.

YIELD: 1½ CUPS

ACTIVE TIME: 5 MINUTES

TOTAL TIME: 5 MINUTES

TAPENADE

1½ CUPS CURED BLACK
OLIVES, PITTED

1 TEASPOON WHITE
MISO PASTE

3 TABLESPOONS
CAPERS, RINSED

1½ TABLESPOONS FINELY
CHOPPED FRESH PARSLEY

3 GARLIC CLOVES

3 TABLESPOONS FRESH
LEMON JUICE

¼ TEASPOON BLACK PEPPER,
PLUS MORE TO TASTE

¼ CUP OLIVE OIL

SALT, TO TASTE

1 Place the olives, miso paste, capers, parsley, garlic, lemon juice, and black pepper in a food processor and pulse until coarsely chopped.

2 Drizzle the olive oil into the mixture and pulse a few more times until a chunky paste forms, scraping down the work bowl as needed. Season with salt and pepper and serve.

YIELD: 3 CUPS

ACTIVE TIME: 25 MINUTES

TOTAL TIME: 2 HOURS

APPLE BUTTER

3 CUPS BRANDY

5 LBS. APPLES, RINSED WELL

½ CUP MAPLE SYRUP

¼ CUP BROWN SUGAR

1 TEASPOON KOSHER SALT

½ TEASPOON CINNAMON

¼ TEASPOON CORIANDER

¼ TEASPOON WHOLE CLOVES

¼ TEASPOON
GROUND NUTMEG

1   Place the brandy in a saucepan and cook over medium-high heat until it has reduced by half. Remove from heat and set aside.

2   Cut the apples into quarters, discard the seeds, place the quarters in a stockpot, and cover with cold water. Bring to a boil over medium-high heat and then reduce the heat so that the water simmers. Cook until the apples are tender, about 15 minutes, and then drain.

3   Preheat the oven to 225°F. Run the apples through a food mill and catch the pulp in a mixing bowl. Add the reduced brandy and the remaining ingredients, stir to combine, and transfer to a shallow baking dish.

4   Place the dish in the oven and bake, while stirring the mixture every 10 minutes until all of the excess water has been evaporated, about 1 to 1½ hours. Remove from the oven, transfer the mixture to a food processor, and puree until smooth. Let the mixture cool completely before using or storing. The apple butter will keep in the refrigerator for up to 2 weeks.

YIELD: 4 SERVINGS
ACTIVE TIME: 5 MINUTES
TOTAL TIME: 10 MINUTES

HONEYED FIGS

6 TABLESPOONS HONEY

16 BLACK MISSION
FIGS, HALVED

½ TEASPOON CINNAMON

GOAT CHEESE, CRUMBLED,
TO TASTE

1   Place the honey in a nonstick skillet and warm over medium heat.

2   When the honey starts to liquefy, place the figs in the skillet, cut-side down, and cook until they start to brown, about 5 minutes.

3   Sprinkle the cinnamon over the figs and gently stir to coat. Remove figs from the pan, top with the goat cheese, and serve.

YIELD: 8 SERVINGS

ACTIVE TIME: 15 MINUTES

TOTAL TIME: 45 MINUTES

GLUTEN-FREE MACAROONS

1¼ CUPS SUGAR

4 CUPS UNSWEETENED SHREDDED COCONUT

4 EGG WHITES

2 TEASPOONS PURE VANILLA EXTRACT

¼ TEASPOON KOSHER SALT

½ CUP SEMISWEET CHOCOLATE CHIPS

1 Preheat the oven to 350°F and line two baking sheets with parchment paper.

2 Place all of the ingredients, except for the chocolate chips, in a mixing bowl and stir until combined. Scoop tablespoons of the mixture onto the baking sheet, making sure to leave room between each scoop.

3 Place in the oven and bake for about 25 minutes, until the macaroons are brown on top. Remove and let cool for about 30 minutes.

4 When the macaroons are almost cool, place the chocolate chips in a microwave-safe bowl and microwave until melted, removing to stir every 15 minutes. Dip the bottoms of the macaroons into the chocolate, place them on wire racks, and let the chocolate set before serving.

YIELD: 16 COOKIES
ACTIVE TIME: 15 MINUTES
TOTAL TIME: 45 MINUTES

CHOCOLATE CHIP COOKIES

14 TABLESPOONS UNSALTED BUTTER

1¾ CUPS ALL-PURPOSE FLOUR

½ TEASPOON BAKING SODA

½ CUP GRANULATED SUGAR

¾ CUP GENTLY PACKED DARK BROWN SUGAR

1 TEASPOON KOSHER SALT

2 TEASPOONS PURE VANILLA EXTRACT

1 LARGE EGG

1 LARGE EGG YOLK

1¼ CUPS SEMISWEET CHOCOLATE CHIPS

1   Preheat the oven to 350°F and line two baking sheets with parchment paper. Place the butter in a saucepan and cook over medium-high heat until it is dark brown and has a nutty aroma. Transfer to a heatproof mixing bowl.

2   Place the flour and baking soda in a mixing bowl and whisk until combined. In the bowl containing the melted butter, add the sugars, salt, and vanilla and beat until combined. Add the egg and egg yolk and beat until the mixture is smooth and thick.

3   Add the dry mixture and stir until incorporated. Fold in the chocolate chips. Form the mixture into 16 balls and place on the parchment-lined baking sheets. Place one sheet of cookies in the oven at a time. Bake, rotating the sheet halfway through, for about 12 minutes, until the cookies are golden brown. Remove from the oven and briefly let cool on the baking sheet before transferring to a wire rack to cool completely.

YIELD: 4 TO 6 SERVINGS

ACTIVE TIME: 20 MINUTES

TOTAL TIME: 45 MINUTES

MILLE-FEUILLE

2 SHEETS OF FROZEN PUFF PASTRY, THAWED

CONFECTIONERS' SUGAR, AS NEEDED

PASTRY CREAM (SEE SIDEBAR)

ZEST OF 1 ORANGE

1 TABLESPOON GRAND MARNIER

1 PINT OF RASPBERRIES

1 Preheat the oven to 400°F. Roll out the sheets of puff pastry and place each one on a greased baking sheet. Dust with confectioners' sugar, place them in the oven, and bake for 12 to 15 minutes, until golden brown. Remove from the oven, transfer to a wire rack, and let cool.

2 Place the Pastry Cream in a bowl, add the orange zest and Grand Marnier, and fold to incorporate. Transfer the mixture into a piping bag and place it in the refrigerator to chill while the puff pastry continues to cool.

3 Divide each sheet of the cooled puff pastry into 3 equal portions. Remove the piping bag from the freezer and place a thick layer of cream on one of the pieces of puff pastry. Dot the edges of the cream with the raspberries and gently press down on them. Fill the space between the raspberries with more of the cream and place another piece of puff pastry on top. Repeat the process with the cream and raspberries and then place the last piece of puff pastry on top. Carefully cut into the desired number of portions and serve.

PASTRY CREAM

1   Place 2 cups whole milk and 1 tablespoon unsalted butter in a saucepan and bring to a simmer over medium heat. As the mixture is coming to a simmer, place ½ cup granulated sugar and 3 tablespoons cornstarch in a small bowl and whisk to combine.

2   Add 2 large eggs and whisk until the mixture is smooth and creamy. While stirring constantly, gradually incorporate half of the milk mixture into the egg mixture. Add a pinch of kosher salt and ½ teaspoon of pure vanilla extract, stir to incorporate, and pour the tempered eggs into the saucepan.

3   Cook, while stirring constantly, until the mixture is thick enough to coat the back of a wooden spoon, making sure not to let it come to a boil. Pour the cream into a bowl, place plastic wrap directly on the surface to prevent a skin from forming, and refrigerate until cool.

YIELD: 12 SQUARES

ACTIVE TIME: 15 MINUTES

TOTAL TIME: 1 HOUR

LEMON SQUARES

1 STICK OF UNSALTED BUTTER

⅓ CUP CONFECTIONERS'
SUGAR

1 CUP ALL-PURPOSE FLOUR,
PLUS 2 TABLESPOONS

PINCH OF KOSHER SALT

2 LARGE EGGS, AT ROOM
TEMPERATURE

1 CUP GRANULATED SUGAR

⅓ CUP FRESH LEMON JUICE

1 TABLESPOON LEMON ZEST

1   Preheat the oven to 350°F and grease a square 8-inch cake pan with nonstick cooking spray.

2   Place the butter, ¼ cup of the confectioners' sugar, the 1 cup of flour, and salt in a mixing bowl and stir until combined. Press the mixture into the baking pan and bake for 20 minutes, or until it is set and lightly browned. Remove from the oven and set aside.

3   Place the eggs, granulated sugar, remaining flour, lemon juice, and lemon zest in a mixing bowl and beat with a handheld mixer until thoroughly combined.

4   Pour the custard over the crust and bake for 20 minutes, or until just browned. The custard should still be soft. Let the pan cool on a wire rack before dusting with the remaining confectioners' sugar and cutting into squares.

GINGERBREAD MADELEINES

5 TABLESPOONS UNSALTED BUTTER, PLUS MORE AS NEEDED

½ CUP GENTLY PACKED BROWN SUGAR

2 EGGS

1 TABLESPOON MINCED GINGER

1¼ TEASPOONS PURE VANILLA EXTRACT

1½ TABLESPOONS MOLASSES

⅓ CUP MILK

½ CUP ALL-PURPOSE FLOUR

½ CUP CAKE FLOUR

¼ TEASPOON BAKING POWDER

1½ TEASPOONS KOSHER SALT

¼ TEASPOON GROUND CLOVES

¼ TEASPOON GRATED FRESH NUTMEG

1 TEASPOON CINNAMON

1   Place the butter in a small saucepan and cook over medium heat until lightly brown. Remove from heat and let cool to room temperature.

2   Place the butter and the brown sugar in a mixing bowl. Beat at medium speed with a handheld mixer fitted with the whisk attachment until light and fluffy. Incorporate the eggs one at a time, and then incorporate the ginger, vanilla, molasses, and milk.

3   Sift the flours and baking powder into a bowl. Add the salt, cloves, nutmeg, and cinnamon and stir to combine. With the mixer running on low, gradually add the dry mixture to the wet mixture and beat until the mixture is a smooth dough. Transfer the dough to the refrigerator and chill for 2 hours.

4   Preheat the oven to 375°F and brush each shell-shaped depression in a madeleine pan with butter. Place the pan in the freezer for at least 10 minutes. Remove the pan from the freezer and the batter from the refrigerator. Fill each "shell" two-thirds of the way with batter and bake until a toothpick inserted into the center of a cookie comes out clean, about 12 minutes. Remove from the oven and place the cookies on a wire rack to cool slightly. Serve warm or at room temperature.

METRIC CONVERSIONS

U.S. Measurement	Approximate Metric Liquid Measurement	Approximate Metric Dry Measurement
1 teaspoon	5 ml	5 g
1 tablespoon or ½ ounce	15 ml	14 g
1 ounce or ⅛ cup	30 ml	29 g
¼ cup or 2 ounces	60 ml	57 g
⅓ cup	80 ml	76 g
½ cup or 4 ounces	120 ml	113 g
⅔ cup	160 ml	151 g
¾ cup or 6 ounces	180 ml	170 g
1 cup or 8 ounces or ½ pint	240 ml	227 g
1½ cups or 12 ounces	350 ml	340 g
2 cups or 1 pint or 16 ounces	475 ml	454 g
3 cups or 1½ pints	700 ml	680 g
4 cups or 2 pints or 1 quart	950 ml	908 g

INDEX

A

ale, Beer Cheese Dip, 160
almonds
    Macarons, 188
    Roasted Almonds, 213
    Spiced Almonds, 24
apples
    Apple Butter, 234
    Baked Apples, 180
apricots
    Apricot & Chili Jam, 96
    Baked Brie, Two Ways, 225
    Dried-Fruit Chutney, 163
    Mostarda, 230
artichokes and artichoke hearts
    Baked Brie, Two Ways, 225
    Pan-Fried Artichokes, 83
asparagus, Asparagus Quiche, 36
avocado, Guacamole, 107

B

bacon
    Bacon Cheese Balls, 47
    Bacon & Zucchini Quiche, 222
Baked Apples, 180
Baked Brie, Two Ways, 225
basil
    Blueberry & Basil Jam, 119
    Pea Shoot Pesto, 52
beans
    Black Bean Hummus, 229
    Dilly Beans, 95
    White Bean Spread, 176
beef
    Cornish Pasties, 34–35
    Runzas, 148
beer
    Stout Bread, 147
    Stout Brownies, 63
beets

Beet Chips, 209
    Roasted Beet Spread, 51
Black Bean Hummus, 229
Black Olive Tapenade, 233
blackberry jam, Baked Apples, 180
blind baking, 36
blue cheese
    Bacon Cheese Balls, 47
    Heavenly Crudité Dip, 104
blueberries
    Blueberry & Basil Jam, 119
    Blueberry Buckle, 124
    Mixed Berry Jam, 120
bread
    Brown Bread, 210
    Cornbread, 92–93
    Crostini with Ricotta & Pea Shoots, 16
    Feta & Herb Bread, 79
    Herb-Crusted Focaccia, 20
    Pita Bread, 23
    Pretzels, 140
    Stout Bread, 147
    See also crackers
Bread & Butter Pickles, 39
Brie, Two Ways, Baked, 225
Brown Bread, 210
Brownies, Stout, 63
bulgur wheat, Tabbouleh, 55
butter
    Cultured Butter, 171
    Herb Butter, 100
buttercreams
    Raspberry Buttercream, 189
    Vanilla Buttercream, 189
butternut squash, Pork Pot Stickers, 138–139

C

cabbage, Runzas, 148
cannellini beans, White Bean Spread, 176

canning 101, 38
Caramelized Onion Mayonnaise, 168
Caraway Water Biscuits, 205
Carrots, Hot & Spicy, 152
cashews, Dudhi Kofta, 31
Cast-Iron Shishito Peppers, 156
cheddar cheese
    Asparagus Quiche, 36
    Bacon Cheese Balls, 47
    Beer Cheese Dip, 160
cheese
    Bacon Cheese Balls, 47
    Beer Cheese Dip, 160
    Cheese Dip, 108
    Cheese Twists, 136
    See also individual types of cheese
cherries, dried
    Baked Brie, Two Ways, 225
    Mostarda, 230
Chestnuts, Roasted, 214
chickpeas, Hummus, 164
Chili Jam, Apricot &, 96
chocolate
    Chocolate Ganache, 189
    Chocolate Soufflé, 64
    Chocolate-Covered Strawberries, 67
    Gluten-Free Macaroons, 238
    Honey Nut Truffles, 187
    Stout Brownies, 63
    Whoopie Pies, 184
Chocolate Chip Cookies, 241
chutneys
    Cilantro & Mint Chutney, 48
    Dried-Fruit Chutney, 163
    Strawberry & Rhubarb Chutney, 44
    See also dips and spreads; jams and jellies
Cilantro & Mint Chutney, 48
Cinnamon Twists, 183
cocoa powder, Whoopie Pies, 184
coconut, Gluten-Free Macaroons, 238

INDEX

cookies
Chocolate Chip Cookies, 241
Gingerbread Madeleines, 246
Gluten-Free Macaroons, 238
Zesty Shortbread, 60
Cornbread, 92–93
Cornish Pasties, 34–35
crackers
Caramelized Onion Mayonnaise, 205
Caraway Water Biscuits, 205
Parmesan Crisps, 15
Rosemary Crackers, 12
Sea Salt & Herb Crackers, 197
See also bread
Cranberry Jam, 179
cream cheese
Beer Cheese Dip, 160
Cheese Dip, 108
Cream Cheese & Radish Dip, 115
Salmon & Dill Quiche, 91
Shiitake Spread, 56
crème fraîche
Asparagus Quiche, 36
Pumpkin Quiche, 151
Crispy Wonton Skins, 135
Crostini with Ricotta & Pea Shoots, 16
cucumbers
Bread & Butter Pickles, 39
Quick Pickles, 155
Spicy Pickles, 80
Tabbouleh, 55
Tzatziki, 112
Cultured Butter, 171

D

daikon radish, Hot & Spicy Carrots, 152
Deep-Fried Oysters, 119
desserts
Baked Apples, 180
Blueberry Buckle, 124
Chocolate Chip Cookies, 241
Chocolate Soufflé, 64

Chocolate-Covered Strawberries, 67
Gingerbread Madeleines, 246
Gluten-Free Macaroons, 238
Honey Nut Truffles, 187
Lemon Squares, 245
Macarons, 188
Mille-Feuille, 242
Miniature Raspberry Tarts, 128
Peach Galette, 127
Rustico with Honey Glaze, 191
Stout Brownies, 63
Sweet Strawberry Pockets, 122-123
Whoopie Pies, 184
Zesty Shortbread, 60
Dill Pickle Arancini, 87
Dilly Beans, 95
dips and spreads
Black Bean Hummus, 229
Black Olive Tapenade, 233
Beer Cheese Dip, 160
Caramelized Onion Mayonnaise, 168
Cheese Dip, 108
Cilantro & Mint Chutney, 48
Cream Cheese & Radish Dip, 115
Cultured Butter, 171
Dried-Fruit Chutney, 163
Eggplant Dip, 172
Eggplant Spread, 40
Guacamole, 107
Heavenly Crudité Dip, 104
Herb Butter, 100
Hot Honey Mustard Dip, 103
Hummus, 164
Lemon-Pepper Mayonnaise, 82
Mostarda, 230
Pea Shoot Pesto, 52
Pork Pâté, 202
Pumpkin Dip, 167
Roasted Beet Spread, 51
Salsa, 116
Shiitake Spread, 56
Strawberry & Rhubarb Chutney, 44

Tzatziki, 112
White Bean Spread, 176
Dudhi Kofta, 31

E

eggplant
Eggplant Dip, 172
Eggplant Spread, 40
eggs
Asparagus Quiche, 36
Bacon & Zucchini Quiche, 222
Pumpkin Quiche, 151
Salmon & Dill Quiche, 91
Southern Deviled Eggs, 201
Spanish Potato Tortilla, 28
Emmental cheese, Fondue, 226
Empanadas, 88–89

F

feta cheese
Feta & Herb Bread, 79
Stuffed Peppers, 76
Stuffed Peppadew Peppers, 198
Tabbouleh, 55
Tiropitakia, 221
figs
Baked Brie, Two Ways, 225
Dried-Fruit Chutney, 163
Honeyed Figs, 237
fish and seafood
Deep-Fried Oysters, 19
Oysters with Mignonette Sauce, 27
Salmon & Dill Quiche, 91
Focaccia, Herb-Crusted, 20
fontina cheese, Cheese Twists, 136
Fondue, 226
fromage blanc, Bacon Cheese Balls, 47

G

Gingerbread Madeleines, 246
Gluten-Free Macaroons, 238

INDEX

goat cheese
  Bacon & Zucchini Quiche, 222
  Baked Apples, 180
  Goat Cheese with Herbs, 43
gouda cheese, Fondue, 226
green beans, Dilly Beans, 95
Green Tomato Jam, 99
Gruyère cheese, Fondue, 226
Guacamole, 107
Guinness
  Stout Bread, 147
  Stout Brownies, 63

H

Havarti cheese, Dill Pickle Arancini, 87
herbs
  Feta & Herb Bread, 79
  Heavenly Crudité Dip, 104
  Herb Butter, 100
  Herb-Crusted Focaccia, 20
  Sea Salt & Herb Crackers, 197
  See also individual herbs
honey
  Honey Nut Truffles, 187
  Honeyed Figs, 237
  Hot Honey, 59
  Rustico with Honey Glaze, 191
Hot & Spicy Carrots, 152
Hot Honey
  Hot Honey Mustard Dip, 103
  recipe, 59
hummus
  Hummus, 164
  Black Bean Hummus, 229

J

jams and jellies
  Apple Butter, 234
  Apricot & Chili Jam, 96
  Blueberry & Basil Jam, 119
  Cranberry Jam, 179
  Green Tomato Jam, 99
  Honeyed Figs, 237
  Mixed Berry Jam, 120
  See also chutneys

K

Kale Chips, 84
kefalotyri cheese, Tiropitakia, 221
Kimchi, 111
Kofta, Dudhi, 31

L

Lemon Curd, 189
Lemon Squares, 245
Lemon-Pepper Mayonnaise
  recipe, 82
  Pan-Fried Artichokes, 83

M

Macarons, 188–189
Macaroons, Gluten-Free, 238
Maple Walnuts, 143
mayonnaise
  Caramelized Onion Mayonnaise, 168
  Heavenly Crudité Dip, 104
  Hot Honey Mustard Dip, 103
  Lemon-Pepper Mayonnaise, 82
Mignonette Sauce, Oysters with, 27
Mille-Feuille, 242
Miniature Raspberry Tarts, 128
mint
  Cilantro & Mint Chutney, 48
  Tabbouleh, 55
Mixed Berry Jam, 120
molasses
  Brown Bread, 210
  Dried-Fruit Chutney, 163
  Gingerbread Madeleines, 246
Mostarda, 230
mozzarella cheese
  Cheese Dip, 108

Rustico with Honey Glaze, 191
mushrooms, Shiitake Spread, 56
Mustard Dip, Hot Honey, 103

N

napa cabbage, Kimchi, 111
nori seaweed, Roasted Seaweed
  Snacks, 218
nuts
  Baked Brie, Two Ways, 225
  Dudhi Kofta, 31
  Macarons, 188
  Roasted Chestnuts, 214
  Spiced Almonds, 24

O

Okra, Pickled, 144
olives
  Baked Brie, Two Ways, 225
  Black Olive Tapenade, 233
  Stuffed Peppers, 76
onions
  Caramelized Onion Mayonnaise, 168
  Empanadas, 88–89
  Onion Rings, 217
  Pork Pâté, 202
  Spicy Pickles, 80
oysters
  Deep-Fried Oysters, 19
  Oysters with Mignonette Sauce, 27

P

Parmesan cheese
  Cheese Twists, 136
  Onion Rings, 217
  Parmesan Crisps, 15
  Pea Shoot Pesto, 52
  Polenta Fries, 32
  Pumpkin Dip, 167
  Pumpkin Quiche, 151
  Shiitake Spread, 56
  Zucchini Fritters, 72

parsley, Tabbouleh, 55

parsnips, Cornish Pasties, 34–35

Pastry Cream

    Mille-Feuille, 242

    recipe, 242

pea shoots

    Crostini with Ricotta & Pea Shoots, 16

    Pea Shoot Pesto, 52

Peach Galette, 127

peanut butter, Honey Nut Truffles, 187

peas, Asparagus Quiche, 36

pecans, Baked Brie, Two Ways, 225

Peppadew Peppers, Stuffed, 198

peppers, bell

    Romesco Sauce, 175

    Spicy Pickles, 80

    Stuffed Peppers, 76

peppers, hot

    Apricot & Chili Jam, 96

    Cast-Iron Shishito Peppers, 156

    Cilantro & Mint Chutney, 48

    Dudhi Kofta, 31

    Guacamole, 107

    Hot Honey, 59

    Pickled Okra, 144

    Roasted Beet Spread, 51

    Salsa, 116

    Salsa Verde, 159

    Spicy Pickles, 80

Peppers, Stuffed Peppadew, 198

Pesto, Pea Shoot, 52

phyllo dough. *See* puff pastry/phyllo dough

Pickled Okra, 144

pickles

    Bread & Butter Pickles, 39

    Dill Pickle Arancini, 87

    Quick Pickles, 155

    Spicy Pickles, 80

piecrust

Asparagus Quiche, 36

Bacon & Zucchini Quiche, 222

blind baking, 36

Miniature Raspberry Tarts, 128

Peach Galette, 127

Pumpkin Quiche, 151

Salmon & Dill Quiche, 91

Sweet Strawberry Pockets, 122–123

pine nuts, Pea Shoot Pesto, 52

Pita Bread, 23

Polenta Fries, 32

pork

    Empanadas, 88–89

    Pork Pâté, 202

    Pork Pot Stickers, 138–139

potatoes

    Cornish Pasties, 34–35

    Purple Potato Chips, 206

    Samosas, 74–75

    Spanish Potato Tortilla, 28

Pretzels, 140

prunes, Dried-Fruit Chutney, 163

puff pastry/phyllo dough

    Cheese Twists, 136

    Cinnamon Twists, 183

    Mille-Feuille, 242

    Rustico with Honey Glaze, 191

    Tiropitakia, 221

pumpkin

    Pumpkin Dip, 167

    Pumpkin Quiche, 151

Purple Potato Chips, 206

Q

quiche

    Asparagus Quiche, 36

    Bacon & Zucchini Quiche, 222

    Pumpkin Quiche, 151

    Salmon & Dill Quiche, 91

Quick Pickles, 155

R

Radish Dip, Cream Cheese &, 115

raisins

    Dried-Fruit Chutney, 163

    Green Tomato Jam, 99

raspberries

    Mille-Feuille, 242

    Miniature Raspberry Tarts, 128

    Mixed Berry Jam, 120

    Raspberry Buttercream, 189

Rhubarb Chutney, Strawberry &, 44

rice, Dill Pickle Arancini, 87

Ricotta & Pea Shoots, Crostini with, 16

Roasted Almonds, 213

Roasted Beet Spread, 51

Roasted Chestnuts, 214

Roasted Seaweed Snacks, 218

Romesco Sauce, 175

rosemary

    Rosemary Crackers, 12

    Zesty Shortbread, 60

Runzas, 148

Rustico with Honey Glaze, 191

S

Salmon & Dill Quiche, 91

salsa

    Salsa, 116

    Salsa Verde, 159

Samosas, 74–75

sauces

    Oysters with Mignonette Sauce, 27

    Romesco Sauce, 175

scallions

    Bacon Cheese Balls, 47

    Kimchi, 111

    Pork Pot Stickers, 139

    Tabbouleh, 55

Sea Salt & Herb Crackers, 197

INDEX

seafood
    Deep-Fried Oysters, 19
    Oysters with Mignonette Sauce, 27
    Salmon & Dill Quiche, 91
Seaweed Snacks, Roasted, 218
Shiitake Spread, 56
smoked salmon, Salmon & Dill Quiche, 91
Soufflé, Chocolate, 64
Southern Deviled Eggs, 201
Spam, Southern Deviled Eggs, 201
Spanish Potato Tortilla, 28
Spiced Almonds, 24
Spicy Pickles, 80
spinach, Cheese Dip, 108
spreads. *See* dips and spreads
stout
    Stout Bread, 147
    Stout Brownies, 63
strawberries
    Chocolate-Covered Strawberries, 67
    Mixed Berry Jam, 120
    Strawberry & Rhubarb Chutney, 44
    Sweet Strawberry Handpies, 122-123
Stuffed Peppadew Peppers, 198
Stuffed Peppers, 76
Sweet Strawberry Handpies, 122-123
Swiss chard, Cheese Dip, 108

T
Tabbouleh, 55
tahini
    Black Bean Hummus, 229
    Hummus, 164
Tapenade, Black Olive, 233
Tiropitakia, 221
tomatillos, Salsa Verde, 159
tomatoes
    Baked Brie, Two Ways, 225
    Empanadas, 88–89
    Green Tomato Jam, 99
    Guacamole, 107
    Romesco Sauce, 175
    Salsa, 116
    Stuffed Peppers, 76
    Tabbouleh, 55
    Tomato Concasse, 106
Tortilla, Spanish Potato, 28
turnips, Cornish Pasties, 34–35
Tzatziki, 112

V
Vanilla Buttercream, 189

W
Walnuts, Maple, 143

White Bean Spread, 176
Whoopie Pies, 184
wine, red, Beer Cheese Dip, 160
wine, white
    Dill Pickle Arancini, 87
    Fondue, 226
    Mostarda, 230
    Strawberry & Rhubarb Chutney, 44
Wonton Skins, Crispy, 135
wrappers, Samosas, 74–75

Y
yogurt
    Cultured Butter, 171
    Feta & Herb Bread, 79
    Pumpkin Dip, 167
    Tzatziki, 112

Z
Zesty Shortbread, 60
zucchini
    Bacon & Zucchini Quiche, 222
    Dudhi Kofta, 31
    Zucchini Fritters, 72

ABOUT CIDER MILL PRESS BOOK PUBLISHERS

Good ideas ripen with time. From seed to harvest, Cider Mill Press brings fine reading, information, and entertainment together between the covers of its creatively crafted books. Our Cider Mill bears fruit twice a year, publishing a new crop of titles each spring and fall.

"Where Good Books Are Ready for Press"

Visit us online at
cidermillpress.com
or write to us at
PO Box 454
12 Spring St.
Kennebunkport, Maine 04046